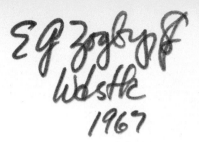

SECULARIZATION THEOLOGY

SECULARIZATION THEOLOGY

ROBERT L. RICHARD, S.J.

HERDER AND HERDER

1967
HERDER AND HERDER NEW YORK
232 Madison Avenue, New York 10016

Imprimi potest: John V. O'Connor, S.J., Provincial
Nihil obstat: Thomas J. Beary, Censor Librorum
Imprimatur: ✠Robert F. Joyce, Bishop of Burlington
May 22, 1967

For permission to include copyrighted material in this volume, the following acknowledgements are gratefully made: to the Daughters of St. Paul for excerpts from Richard Cardinal Cushing's Pastoral Letter *The Servant Church,* of Gaudete Sunday, December, 1966, © 1966 by the Daughters of St. Paul; to the Macmillan Company for excerpts made from *The Secular City Debate,* edited by Daniel Callahan, © 1966 by The Macmillan Company, and from *The Secular City,* by Harvey Cox, © 1965 by Harvey Cox, and from *The Secular Meaning of the Gospel,* by Paul van Buren, © 1963 by Paul van Buren; and to Westminster Press for excerpts from *Honest to God,* by John A. T. Robinson, © 1963 by SCM Publishers.

Contents

Contents

Foreword

"What is striking about Dr. Robinson's book is first and foremost that he is an atheist." With these words non-believer Alasdair MacIntyre tried to locate believing Bishop John A. T. Robinson, author of *Honest to God,* in the camp of non-belief.

"What is striking about Father Richard's book is first and foremost that he is a protestant." With these words the undersigned Protestant is trying to locate the Catholic Robert L. Richard, S.J., author of *Secularization Theology,* in the camp of protestantism.

Not really. My characterization is no more accurate than was MacIntyre's. The difference is this: MacIntyre may have been trying to be fair to Robinson; I have not even tried with Richard. My interest in being unfair to Father Richard in my own inimitably biased fashion lies in the desire to accent the strongest and at the same time the weakest feature of this important study.

Try again: another way to put it might be to suggest that Father Richard has written the first volume of a two-volume work. He is not working on that volume, to the best of my knowledge; he may not even know that he is to write it. But his work will not be finished until he does a "catholic" sequel.

Before the heresy-hunters or their analogues in the post-Vatican Council era, the yellow journalists of the "right," take up their pursuit of him, let me explain that *Secularization Theology* is a protestant book with a lower-case "p" and not with the formidable capitalized "P" that signifies an institutional element in Christ's Church. In other words, his book has picked up a legitimate dimension of the Catholic tradition. He shares with a number of Protestant thinkers of our time a concern that the prophetic note be sounded, that the resources of the Church be exercised in the tasks of exorcism, iconoclasm, and the purging of the false.

He does not reside in a half-way house to Protestantism; he is already protestant by his commitment to the task of helping the world move beyond magic and alchemy and superstition, beyond enslaving religiousness that has not let itself hear the word of Jesus Christ.

In the compass of this brief volume he introduces readers to a two-decade-long episode in Christian thought, an episode in which Protestant Christians were the noisy agents but in which they are now joined by notable Roman Catholics. This episode saw the formation of a school of thought which we might denominate as "Secular Theology." It is no longer struggling for acceptance against orthodoxy or neo-orthodoxy; it *is* the prevailing new orthodoxy. Perhaps it is past its prime. Historians like to observe that systems and codifications of thought or summaries of movements begin to become possible when a movement or a ferment is past: after the closing of the frontier or after the abolition of slavery historians began to be able to write histories of the frontier and of slavery. After secular theology we can begin to write books like *Secularization Theology.*

Not that the act of becoming acquainted with post-World War II thought ("from Bonhoeffer through Robinson and van Buren and Cox to Hamilton") is a waste of time. If that were so, there would be no point in commending it to readers in a foreword to a book such as this one. Rather it has become time to consolidate some gains, appreciate some achievements, and organize some insights, so that a new generation can find its own theological language appropriate to the needs of the Church.

Those who know the Secular Theology tradition well can read *Secularization Theology* in order to compare notes and viewpoints and to discern Father Richard's clues for the catholic future. Those who have not done their homework will find here a succinct cram course, one which almost overwhelms the reader with its allusive references by the time the author is writing the third paragraph of the Preface. Be patient: as the book proceeds he goes into great and helpful detail about the people he introduces so briskly at the beginning.

Father Richard makes clear that he agrees in the main with the secularizing theologians. For centuries man has been progressively asserting his domain over the world; he has been purging it (and himself) of the spooky elements which had kept him in bondage; he has radically changed his attitude toward the whole of reality; he has found it possible to think of religion in the old ways only at the expense of his full humanity and of the surrender of the Lordship of Jesus Christ. "The world" knew all but the last of these historical strophes for a long time; in our time the Church is trying to learn them all, indeed to seize initiative and—in some senses—to lead in the pace of secularization. All in the name of God.

God? There is the problem! For these theologians have discovered that even the name and concept of God have not been exempted from examination; they have not been exiled to a safe precinct. Father Richard repeatedly and unerringly finds his magnetic needle pointing to a pole marked "the problem of God." He is on the verge of sharing the secularizers' oversimplified view of Jesus, but his catholic heart tells him that he cannot do this without making an idol of the man Jesus. He must somehow relate Jesus Christ to "transcendence" or some equivalent concept. Toward that pole the magnetic needles of all the theologians today are pointing; some are fixed there and others still engage in the nervous dance that compass-needles like to show us.

Further than this Father Richard does not take us. He carries us to the brink of the issues raised by Bernard Lonergan or Leslie Dewart or (surprise!) Richard Cardinal Cushing. In doing so he may frustrate some readers: why do the theologians always tell us what the problem now is instead of addressing themselves to new words which might help solve it?

Human freedom-talk without Jesus-talk is unsatisfying and cannot be considered Christian. Jesus-talk without God-talk is idolatrous. Yet God-talk is problematic. The secular theologians know the first and the third of these propositions best. They have chosen an urgent and difficult part of the theological task for our time. But, as Father Richard makes amply clear, they are coming to know that the problem of God and of transcendence has to be faced. Theology is not only protest against the false gods; it is the celebration of the True. That celebration is a catholic concern, and Father Richard, in tiptoeing to the point of it, has served us well as a guide but left himself with that agenda item: the writing of the "catholic" volume two. If he follows through, he will have won our confidence on the basis of this balanced and provocative work.

MARTIN E. MARTY

Preface

THE BONHOEFFER-oriented *Secularization of Christianity* may someday prove to have been—despite its apparent negativism—one of the truly creative religious movements of modern times. This is a possibility, however, not as yet a fact. The movement, like that of the *Death of God* with which, at least at the popular level, it is all mixed up, could also prove to have been little more than a flash in the theological pan.

But right away, simply by mentioning the link between *Secularization* and *Death of God,* we put a finger on the real problem in all of this, that of genuine intellectual identity.

At the present moment, there is talk first of all of the *New Radical Theology.* By itself, the rubric would not be especially informative. In context, however, the designation seems intended to include any contemporary theologian or theological group speculating on the other-than-Bultmannian radical fringe and challenging even the few and far between traditionalist presuppositions of the Bultmannians. Thus one thinks immediately of every present-day theologian who has attached himself to Bonhoeffer's insistence that Bultmann and *demythologizing* do not go anywhere near far enough in coping with the ultimate problem of being able to say anything at all about "God": of Paul van Buren, therefore, and John A. T. Robinson, perhaps also of Harvey Cox and even the Roman Catholic Leslie Dewart. But one thinks also of the *Death of God* group, if it really is a group, who do not (except for Hamilton, and he, it would appear, not too seriously) depend upon Bonhoeffer, but who very much like to identify themselves as the *New Radical Theologians:* of William Hamilton, therefore, and Thomas J. J. Altizer, and possibly also, though in this case the identification has been made rather by others than the man himself, of Gabriel Vahanian. It remains, however, that as a classification *New Radical Theologian* is at best a very vague and clumsy intellectual identity.

Does *Death of God,* then, enjoy more success? At the moment, it seems no, or at least not very much so. For example, a name currently associated with the inside of a *Death of God* movement, Vahanian's, will not unlikely be crossed off altogether, to be entered rather with that Christian Existentialism against which much of the new theology is largely in reaction. Another name now and then on the same *Death of God* list, Cox's, will likewise probably be removed once and for all, but only, as is certainly possible, that it might henceforth head the list more appropriately styled *Secularized Christianity.* This would leave Altizer, Hamilton and van Buren. The last mentioned, however, does not want to be taken as a *Death of God* spokesman, and in any case his empiricist secularizationism (to avoid confusion with the doctrinaire secularism which van Buren disavows) moves in a largely opposite direction from Altizer's emphasis on the sacred, albeit that it is a this-worldly sacred. If one erases from the list people who probably never belonged there in the first place, and then people who much more accurately would be classified under *Secularized Christianity,* there does not seem to be much left of *Death of God* except Altizer and Hamilton. But even the latter shows some signs of greater affinity with the Bonhoeffer *Secularization* movement than with the Altizer with whom he is commonly paired. And so, as a matter of fact, it would not be surprising if *Death of God* came eventually to be reserved for the Altizer-style mythology of God's "death" that is more immediately linked to the original and strictly Nietzschean proclamation: "God is dead!" But neither would it be surprising if such a school actually failed to develop and "death of God" dropped once again into theology's back pages. In our judgment, it is too early to tell whether the Altizer *Death of God* is likely to turn out sufficiently distinctive and productive in its valid insights.

Quite a more positive assessment seems justified, however, in the case of the remaining possibility, *Secularization of Christianity*. For some, of course, the *Secularization of Christianity* movement is simply a *Death of God* sub-group, but we have already shown, at least briefly, that this is due to hasty advertising at the level of the newspaper kiosks and the desire to make the most of a very striking and challenging title. In point of fact, the *Secularization* movement is distinct, and this will be brought out more clearly as we study the many ways in which such a movement has already succeeded in defining itself as a genuine intellectual identity.

To anticipate what will be demonstrated later on, we might observe that the intellectual identity which we are discussing has at least four marks by which it may be known. First, it consistently owes its inspiration, though perhaps a good deal less of its detail, to Dietrich Bonhoeffer and the now famous plea for a "secularized" Christianity. Secondly, and in this continuing to echo Bonhoeffer's own thought, it is always in some sense decidedly Christocentric. Thirdly, again as an implication contained in the Bonhoeffer manifesto, it exhibits the common trait of wishing to remove from Christianity, at least in some qualified sense and in some limited measure, a traditional emphasis on the "other-worldly." Fourthly and finally, and still in the steps of Bonhoeffer who contested that Bultmann rather than going too far had not gone far enough, it desires to come to grips, honestly and unafraid, with what is most absolutely basic in the long-taken-for-granted language of "belief" in "God." It should be noted in passing, moreover, that when these four marks are thus broadly phrased and qualified they actually and accurately describe such widely separated *Secularization* statements as, at one extreme, Paul van Buren's *The Secular Meaning of the Gospel*—ranging through Bishop John Robinson's *Honest to God* and Harvey Cox's *The Secular City* in what we might call the middle—and Richard Cardinal Cushing's pastoral letter *The Servant Church*.

In contemporary theology, however, and given the dialectical thrust of present-day thought, identification is most easily achieved through confrontation. It is high time that traditionalist theologians, or if not necessarily favoring the term "traditionalist" at least such as do not belong to the unrestricted radicalism of the moment, entered into serious book-length conversation with the latter in an effort to engage gradually emerging issues. Such was clearly the intention of Eric Mascall in his scholarly critique called, as a matter of fact, *The Secularization of Christianity*.

Quite deliberately, Mascall limited the scope of his study to the new radical theology of van Buren and Robinson, and to the single issue of *reductionism* so manifestly raised in both of these authors. This was, then, a specific, long overdue and theologically significant beginning. Mascall, an Anglican theologian of strong Thomist sympathies, found that the reductionist exegesis of van Buren and Robinson rather gratuitously assumed that there was no intelligent, strictly modern, alternative to such an exegesis for coping with the linguistic and philosophical problems inherent in the Christian revelation. This was too much. It evidenced, moreover, a cavalier, thoroughly un-modern disregard for the contemporary intellectual and scientific dialogue. Mascall, therefore, set about a point by point examination, and for the greater part refutation, of the reductionist argument. It was based, in the final analysis, on an altogether too neat assumption of what "modern man," intellectually and scientifically "come of age," simply had to take for granted. Confrontation was at least in progress.

It is upon this foundation that the present writer would like to build. He agrees with Mascall that reductionism is a serious issue in van Buren, and to a lesser degree in Robinson. But before, as it were, leaving the subject, we want to suggest that in certain key spots the biblical and systematic theology with which Mascall attempts to engage reductionism might itself be further nuanced, in a sense brought more up to date. For we are not entirely satisfied that Mascall's own treatment of either "historic factuality" in the biblical context, or "objective reality" in the philosophical, really meets the challenge of reductionists. We likewise, and more importantly, want to suggest that there is another and more creative issue gradually clarifying in the *Secularization* theology—even in van Buren and Robinson. This is what might be called the historical, sociocultural, religious and moral "law" of evolutionary optimism.

I.

The Genealogy and the Message

A. The Genealogy

THE PRESENT-DAY Secularization of Christianity movement, like any other, has a traceable parentage, even though the parentage this time is quite complex, and made rather the more so by the fact that the identity of the offspring is also somewhat complex. In *Honest to God*, Bishop John Robinson gets into his extraordinarily popular little book by naming, towards the end of his first chapter, the three writings of three well-known theologians from the generation preceding which contained "ideas that immediately found lodgement when [he] first read them and which have since proved seminal not only for [him] but for many of this generation." The progenitors: Paul Tillich, Dietrich Bonhoeffer, Rudolf Bultmann.

Robinson's triad makes a good place to start. But it will be more convenient to change his order to Bultmann, Tillich, Bonhoeffer. For in the first place, any discussion whatsoever of a new radical theology will automatically remind the informed audience of the role of Bultmann in the generation just past, and just as automatically raise the question of a natural continuity. Few names were more prominent than his in the development and spread of yesterday's quite radical Christian Existentialism, and no name more prominent in the even more radical New Testament reinterpretation with which Christian Existentialism became closely allied. Secondly, it seems proper to end with Bonhoeffer. Compared with Bultmann and Tillich, what Bonhoeffer left behind was relatively little, and still less if we limit our consideration to what within that little is immediately pertinent to the Secularization movement of today. Yet, it is Bonhoeffer, not Bultmann or Tillich, who has truly, even if at the same time a bit mysteriously, fathered this movement.

But first we must see what Robinson makes of Bultmann. Robinson, as he tells us himself, was not really struck by the relevance of *Kerygma and Myth* until it was translated into English in 1953. We have to remember, however, that he was a biblical theologian by trade, and that in such a capacity he would have been aware of the Bultmann debate, and tuned in on its Continental wave length, more or less all along. In any case, the first point to consider apropos of Bultmann's part in the genesis of John Robinson's theology, and perhaps that of the other secularizers, is that here the newer current of thought has its link to modern biblical theology and New Testament exegesis. The second point to consider in the same context is that here again the new radicalism also has its link to post-World War II Christian Existentialism.

The importance of this observation on the role of Bultmann is not at all that today's radicalism develops as either biblical theology or Christian Existentialism. As a matter of fact, this is precisely what it does not do. In the writer's judgment, and allowing for a measure of exception in the methodology employed by the *Death of God* theologian Thomas J. J. Altizer, the new radical theology is most emphatically not a biblical theology. Certainly, and despite superficial impressions to the contrary, the Secularization theology is not. And this, incidentally, is the reason why the conclusions of the Secularization movement and, in fact, of the entire new theology cannot ultimately be coped with by biblical theology left to itself. The discussion has to be moved to a philosophically wider base. Nor, by much the same token, is the new radical theology a further statement, or sum of statements, in the evolution of Christian Existentialism. Rather, in Paul van Buren and even, though to a lesser extent, in Harvey Cox, one of the things that stand out most prominently is the reaction *against* Christian Existentialism.

Biblical theology, on the other hand, and the Christian Existentialism with which it is interlocked, constitute the two great pre-*Death of God* and Secularization of Christianity movements in contemporary Christian thought. Hence, if the Bultmann link is Secularization's only link with these two earlier and more established movements, the same Bultmann link is Secularization's only point of contact with the up-to-now main line of the modern Christian dialogue. It is important, therefore, to see how much (or how little) the Secularization movement actually owes to Bultmann.

Robinson himself, as we have noted, is explicit. He acknowledges an influence of Bultmann's demythologizing exegesis and the effort to reinterpret the New Testament for present-day man upon his own personal theological quest, and he attributes a similar Bultmann influence to others. The bishop, however, may be a man with an idea, who is looking for a footnote. More accurately, he may be simply trying to assign credit for one of the major insights of modern theology, an insight which he, and those with whom he identifies himself, have long ago taken for granted, and have absorbed into their own, perhaps now quite different, thinking. There is an indication of something like this in Robinson's remark on the "air of old-fashioned modernism" in Bultmann's cavalier appeal to the certainties of "scientific dogmatism" in his process of demythologizing. It is as if to say, "He made his point, though of course . . ."

Bultmann's light was that we have in the New Testament kerygma an invitation to authentic existence, that his invitation must be made relevant to the man of today, but that it cannot possibly be made so unless the total message is purified, "demythologized," of all its mythological objectifications. Angels coming down to earth from heaven above and bearing divine communications, a virgin conceiving miraculously, an incarnation of a son of God—none of this can the intelligent man of the twentieth century, scientifically and philosophically oriented, even begin any longer to take at face value. It has to go. Once it is removed, then the underlying profoundly simple and existential meaning of the New Testament can once again be declared and lived.

Now there is something here that the entire new radical theology has assimilated: the principle that the New Testament cannot in any case simply be "repeated," but must first be pressed to learn what it really "means." It must be demythologized. But demythologizing is actually an earlier form of "reductionism"— that reductionism which Eric Mascall in his *Secularization of Christianity* singles out as the one outstanding common feature of the more recent movement.

Already in the fore-evening of the newer theology, however, Dietrich Bonhoeffer had challenged Bultmann that demythologizing was not enough. Robinson quotes with enthusiasm the well-known passage in *Letters and Papers from Prison*. Looking back on Bultmann's original essay, Bonhoeffer commented not that Bultmann "went too far, as most people seem to think, but that he did not go far enough. It is not only the mythological conceptions, such as the miracles, the ascension and the like (which are not in principle separable from the conceptions of God, faith and so on) that are problematic, but the 'religious' conceptions themselves. You cannot, as Bultmann imagines, separate God and miracles, but you do have to be able to interpret and proclaim *both* of them in a 'non-religious' sense." Bonhoeffer's reductionism, then, would not only have gone further than Bultmann's, but would have taken a decisively different turn. Bultmann never dreamed of demythologizing God. Bon-hoeffer did. And in his *Secular Meaning of the Gospel*, van Buren feels that he has performed the task.

Van Buren's early studies under Barth had brought him, too, into the ambient of the Bultmann debate. Undoubtedly, de-mythologizing suggested an opening and a methodological point of departure for his own strongly rationalist reflexions. But van Buren, like Bonhoeffer, found demythologizing unsatisfactory. The ultimate problem in the New Testament, and in any re-ligious utterance, was language—beginning with the little piece of language that is "God." Demythologizing had missed this completely. Van Buren's reductionist theology, therefore, would apply instead methods of linguistic analysis, and try to come to terms not only with the talk, however mythological, *about* God, but with God (or "God"—i.e., the piece of language) himself. For contrary to what Bultmann and demythologizing had presumed, the two could not be separated.

Thus, quite understandably, van Buren's *Secular Meaning of the Gospel* makes extremely little positive use of Bultmann. His criticism of Bultmann, on the other hand, is extensive. Yet, as we shall have occasion to point out at somewhat greater length in the chapter following, for all van Buren's impatience with the Bultmannian solution, van Buren himself has clearly in-corporated the central Bultmannian insight, and this is quite significant in its own right.

Harvey Cox's *Secular City*, if we except the bibliography, con-tains only a single reference to Bultmann, and that not to de-mythologizing. On the other hand, in Cox, just as in van Buren, there are signs throughout that the *elementum bultmannianum* exerts an influence at least as something long since assimilated and henceforth taken for granted. Such influence, however, would not suffice to make Bultmann the parent of the newer theology, and it is but a tribute to Bultmann that the same in-fluence can be discovered among countless other modern theologians who have really little or nothing to do with the precise newer theology that we are discussing.

Now thus far, we have been considering the Bultmann contribution from the specific viewpoint of the demythologizing exegesis. It is necessary, therefore, before leaving the subject of Bultmann, to give equally specific consideration to the Christian Existentialism which became wedded to the Bultmannian exegesis in the phase of reinterpretation.

And it is likewise yes and no with Secularization's dependence, and the dependence of the entire new radical theology, upon Christian Existentialism. Speaking about "worldly holiness" in the latter part of *Honest to God,* Robinson lets himself be guided chiefly by Bonhoeffer. "The Christian life, the life of 'the man for others,' must, as Bonhoeffer insisted, be a 'worldly' life. Yet it must be a life of 'holy worldliness', of 'sacred secularity'." In the same section, Robinson reverts to a theme which he had labored earlier, and strives to combine with this "sacred secularity" the Tillichian ideal of conceiving God in depth, rather than in distance. As Robinson interprets Tillich, Tillich the Existentialist and Bonhoeffer the Secularist come together at this point: Tillich's reinterpretation of transcendence puts God back on earth, or *in* earth, in the depth of the human condition and as man's ultimate concern. But Robinson does not make similar use here of Bultmann's "authentic existence." His style of speech, however, has nevertheless absorbed the primary existentialist categories. He is quite preoccupied with interpersonalism, with encounter, with engagement, even as, significantly, he gives each of these a new and secularist thrust. Once more, therefore, something from the earlier dialogue has at least become assimilated and continues to exercise an influence, though now from afar.

Van Buren, for his part, actually flays against the whole spirit of contemporary Christian Existentialism, and especially as this spirit motivates the New Testament reconstructions of Bultmann and Schubert Ogden. The latter position, in van Buren's appraisal, "has not done justice to the historical aspect of the Gospel." But also, and more immediately in point, "even in its attempt to be 'modern,' it has not done justice to the secular, empirical spirit of our age." "Modern" man, for van Buren, is, we must bear in mind, "empirically minded" man, and in many ways he is the neat antithesis of his existentialist forerunner. No less than Robinson, however, and certainly with a more consciously deliberate use of words, van Buren himself has taken over what he presumes to have been of permanent value in the existentialist insights. His own key notion of "discernment situation" (borrowed from Ian Ramsey), for example, obviously builds upon what was a basic supposition of the existentialist psychology. Still more existential, is his use of the concept of freedom. Finally, van Buren's technical quarrel with Bultmann and Ogden is not that the New Testament kerygma contains no statements which are "plainly existential," but that it contains others which are "empirical as well."

Cox sees Christian Existentialism, even its Tillichian fringe, as already *passé*. "Both philosophical existentialism and Paul Tillich's theology are expressions of the mourning period which began with the death of the God of metaphysical theism and Western civilization, but the wake is now over. That is why existentialist theologies and philosophies do not partake of the spirit of the emerging age but symbolize rather the passing of the old." Nevertheless, Cox's own religious ideal remains in its broadest features that of a now pragmatized, secularized, perhaps we should say "professionalized" and made "career-worthy," involvement. Cox's sociological theology is a far-reaching corrective of existentialism. The involvement has been stripped of its self-consciousness, and its inclination to time-wasting romantic rhapsody. It has become brisk, purposeful, down to earth and matter of fact. In the best sense, and best spiritual sense, of the word, it gets things done. As a corrective of existentialism, moreover, it by no means grew out of existentialism either exclusively or even primarily: no more than did the culture of megalopolis. Yet, at least one of its many roots was, and therefore in a fashion remains, the spontaneous sympathy with existentialism's avowedly uncompromising goal of the relevant, authentic and totally committed personal existence.

The new theology's break with Christian Existentialism, with the specifically Bultmannian and with that which was simply in the air of the times, is, then, rather more decisive than its break with demythologizing as such; though again there was something to be assimilated before taking leave. There is a fundamental tension today between the entire new radical theology and Christian Existentialism, a tension that is brought out very sharply in the literary essays of Gabriel Vahanian's *Wait Without Idols*. Vahanian, in fact, though popularly listed as a *Death of God* theologian, sounds much more like a *Death of God* observer and commentator than advocate. The nostalgia is patent. His sympathies lie with the Christian Existentialism that is being displaced.

All in all, therefore, the new theology's link to Bultmann, to the exegetical method and more especially to the existentialist reinterpretation, is somewhat nebulous. Bultmann's role has been largely that of providing dialectical point of departure. In no serious sense can he be called the father of either the Secularization movement or *Death of God*.

As for Paul Tillich, to go on, Robinson himself makes much of him, every bit as much as he makes of Bonhoeffer. But we should note the context. In his third chapter, given the Tillichian title "The Ground of Our Being," Robinson introduces Tillich to help rid the discussion of all the nonsense about the God "up there" and "out there." "This, I believe, is Tillich's great contribution to theology—the reinterpretation of transcendence in a way which preserves its reality while detaching it from the projection of supranaturalism."

Tillich's theology, however, is so methodologically sophisticated and epistemologically nuanced, that the bishop's summary makes the Tillich of *Honest to God* a Tillich at the surface. Reinhold Niebuhr, according to a remark made by him in his interview with Ved Mehta reported in *The New Yorker,* November 13, 1965, apparently feels the same way.

Van Buren, for his part, makes only three references to Tillich, and none of these affects the central thrust of his own argument.

Cox, on the other hand, banishes Tillich altogether. "Like existentialism, which is its formal philosophical expression, the 'ultimate question' Tillich wants us all to ask arises from Western man's realization that the Hegelian synthesis held no title to foundation in reality, that Christian civilization was gone and that its God was dead. Tillich's life spans the years of this frightening realization, and he speaks with unparalleled power to those whose spiritual life is defined by the same transition. He is thus the theologian's theologian, the indispensable comforter of those who grew up in a faith they can no longer believe. But today's urban-secular man has not lived through this loss of innocence. He was never innocent to begin with."

A wider and certainly more sympathetic treatment of Tillich, we might note in passing, is incorporated into Altizer's *Mircea Eliade and the Dialectic of the Sacred.* But Altizer, who makes no use of Bonhoeffer whatsoever (except to challenge the inadequacies of "the persistent calls for a 'religionless Christianity'" in his more recently published *The Gospel of Christian Atheism*), is not working for Secularization in the first place, at least not in the sense of the Bonhoeffer tradition.

What, finally, of Bonhoeffer's own role? In a way, it is difficult to judge. He had written, after all, so very little on the matter. Yet, when the question as to how much today's Secularization movement actually depends upon Dietrich Bonhoeffer is asked, the most accurate reply would seem to be the paradoxical one: in relatively little, and still in almost everything.

Van Buren brings this out quite clearly. On the one hand, his references to Bonhoeffer are comparatively few, and all but one —an important one, however: the citation of Bonhoeffer's summary of the characteristics of religion in the *Ethics*—are taken from the posthumous *Letters and Papers from Prison,* and from the brief final section of the volume at that. On the other hand, the very opening paragraph of *The Secular Meaning of the Gospel* is van Buren's personal translation of the now famous passage in the *Letters:* " 'Honesty demands that we recognize that we must live in the world as if there were no God. And this is just what we do recognize—before God! God himself drives us to this realization. —God makes us know that we must live as men who can get along without Him. The God who is with us is the God who foresakes us (Mark 15:34)! We stand continually in the presence of the God who makes us live in the world without the God-hypothesis'." The rest of van Buren's study will be, at least in the author's intention, an attempt to implement in detail the theological program which Bonhoeffer's words suggested. Towards the end of the book, van Buren himself says as much, but at the same time intimates that only the root idea could be taken from Bonhoeffer directly. "As we said at the very beginning," van Buren writes, "Bonhoeffer hoped that a 'non-religious interpretation of biblical concepts' would both overcome the weakness of liberal theology and at the same time do justice to its legitimate question. Our method is one which never occurred to Bonhoeffer, but our interpretation may nonetheless serve to justify his hope."

Somewhat similarly, Cox makes very little specific appeal to Bonhoeffer's writings, and with only two exceptions, one of which is merely a general reference to the *Ethics,* these are again to the last section of the *Letters.* But likewise somewhat similarly, Cox both begins and ends *The Secular City* by describing his own reflexions as an attempt to accept the challenge, and develop the simply stated but extraordinary suggestion of Bonhoeffer.

And it is the same with Robinson. In *Honest to God,* Robinson explicitly notes the necessity of examining Bonhoeffer's earlier works in order fully to appreciate the remarks in the *Letters;* yet in the same book he admits in another place that he has been able to concentrate only on these latter. Nonetheless, the Bonhoeffer plea for a secular way of talking about God and a worldly holiness in identification with the career of Jesus as essentially "the man for others" has almost certainly been Robinson's chief inspiration.

In general, then, perhaps "inspiration" is all that can safely be said, but perhaps that is saying a great deal. In our opinion, the tendency of some today to dismiss the claimed influence of Bonhoeffer as sentimentalism is just as uncritical as the opposite tendency to exaggerate the impact precisely on our new radical theology of the greater detail of Bonhoeffer's life's work.

At this point, it seems that we can summarize the role of Robinson's three heroes, and append some further observations of our own on the matter of genealogy and immediate background. First, there is a measure of original dependence upon Bultmann's demythologizing, and there is ample evidence for an assimilation of many of the cardinal insights of Christian Existentialism. But the demythologizing has been given a decisively new direction, and the existentialist insights have been so thoroughly transformed that a main characteristic of the more recent movements is that their spirit is now really in direct opposition to the existentialist. Secondly, there is a take-over, at least in Robinson himself, of an immanentist principle discovered in Tillich. But beyond that, Tillich's role is actually minimal, and in Cox even a point of conflict and departure. Finally, there does remain the profound initiating influence of Bonhoeffer.

But there is something else, too. When the theologian-reader gets into *The Secular City,* especially in Part Two and Part

Three, he may suddenly begin to feel the well-known symptoms of footnote fatigue. (We ourself freely admit that we did.) He may not recognize a number of the names, and he may begin to wonder how some of them can thus be made active participants in a supposedly theological dialogue. The Roman Catholic theologian-reader, unfortunately, will experience this malaise more than others. As a quite general rule, while he may well know—today—that there is a "modern" theology, he does not know—yet—that there is an "American" theology, or even an "Anglo-Saxon" theology.

His "modern" theology is almost exclusively a Continental import. And what prevents him, ordinarily, from recognizing a distinctly "American" theology is that much of American theology, just like American philosophy, is practiced in the presumably non-theological, and non-philosophical, world of sociology, social psychology, economics, cultural history and several other allied disciplines. But this lack of recognition is regrettable. For it is precisely in the broadly sociological area, largely though not exclusively American, that the far more significant dependence of Harvey Cox really lies: it seems that Cox's first insight was to have realized that this is where the Bonhoeffer program would have its best, and perhaps only, chance for implementation.

Something of the same is also true of Paul van Buren, though now the precise area will be linguistics rather than social science. The primary dependence of *Secular Meaning of the Gospel* is upon Anthony Flew, Ian T. Ramsay, R. M. Hare and R. B. Braithwaite—upon what a typically American and Roman Catholic theologian is going to consider the non-theological certainly, and at least sub-philosophical, school of the British linguistic analysts.

An interesting observation, therefore, could be inserted here before concluding this brief sketch of the Secularization genealogy.

It is not without significance that van Buren found demythologizing unsatisfactory, and for different or at least more precise
reasons than Bonhoeffer, and that he abandoned Bultmann for
the Anglo-Saxon, chiefly British, linguistic analysts. Nor is it
without significance that Cox's itinerary has been, though less
exclusively, via an equally Anglo-Saxon, this time chiefly American, religious sociology. For as van Buren himself notes explicitly, and Robinson likewise, this new radical theology is very
much an Anglo-Saxon phenomenon. What it most immediately
departs from, on the other hand, demythologizing and existentialist reinterpretation, is not Anglo-Saxon, but Continental and
mostly German.

This is not the time, obviously, to stir up any fires of nationalistic adherence. Nor could anything be more directly opposed to the spirit of the Secularization movement. But it may
be the time to talk a bit of common sense. Nationalism would
have no place in a theological discussion, unless the discussion
were taken up with the moral problem of nationalism, just as
it might be taken up with the moral problem of racism, precisely. But cultural heritage does have a place in theological
discussion, inasmuch as it is vital to the questions of language
and meaning.

There are two further considerations that prompt the writer
to observe, as Van Buren and Robinson have done before him,
the peculiarly Anglo-Saxon character of the current movement,
and to do so with far less fear than he might have felt in the
past of being misunderstood in his intention.

First, the generation coming along, the post-Vatican II generation with which men like Robinson and Cox are so strongly
identified, is by and large unaffected by the nationalistic spirit
that continued, for all the politeness, to harass their elders. This
shows, in our opinion, in the music and dance forms to which
today's teenager and young adult is so much attached. It seems,
in fact, that the language of the *discs* is really the first successful

international communication this world has seen. Whatever this language may be saying, and we shall not risk a guess, it is saying the same thing—in New York or London, in Paris or Rome or Berlin, in Prague or Moscow. And it is the same in the academic world of ideas in which these young people are just now growing up. Such has been our personal experience teaching in an international seminary. It makes little difference—today —whether the idea belongs to a Frenchman or a German, an Italian or a Spaniard, an Englishman or an American—so long as it is an idea, an idea they can appreciate as "meaningful" and "relevant." But paradoxically, just because this is their sentiment, because the bars of nationalistic sensitiveness and one-up-manship are being broken through, they no longer see a need to suppress in an artificial manner cultural differences. The language of the discs, in fact, even accentuates these differences, and does so without embarrassment. It is one of the more wholesome and holy traits of the emerging secular city.

Secondly, where the Secularization of Christianity is in question, the genesis of this movement exhibits a truly extraordinary and edifying degree of *inter*national cross-fertilization. Van Buren's theological formation was completed under Barth at Basle. Cox, who had earlier enjoyed direct personal experience of the German situation, later returned to Germany as a mature scholar, to spend a further year in what seems to have been intense intellectual and pastoral involvement. Robinson's list of progenitors is at least a list of three famous German theologians. But two of the three are Tillich and Bonhoeffer: the Tillich who came to make America his second home, and the Bonhoeffer who was able to experience firsthand the specifically Anglo-Saxon and American urban technopolis before returning to his native Germany and giving thought in prison to how modern man might come to "speak in a secular fashion of God." And Bonhoeffer, if neither Bultmann nor Tillich, does have the right to be styled the father of the movement. If the movement is

Anglo-Saxon, therefore, it can be anything but nationalistically so.

On the other hand, and with equal candor, we must note that it is culturally so. What it assimilates from non-Anglo-Saxon cultures, on the Continent and especially in Germany, it has nevertheless given a distinctly Anglo-Saxon final turn. In our judgment—referring for a moment to the United States, and especially to Roman Catholic theology in the United States— this observation is quite important. For without that final turn, theology, no theology, can discourse successfully with the American secular city—not even with its Roman Catholics. The existentialist categories that have so largely overtaken American Catholic theology may have become very useful and meaningful for those who have had long experience of them, in the original or at least in American translation. But by and large they are not the categories in which America's scientific technological and secular humanist will ever learn to talk comfortably about God.

B. The Message

In present-day Academe, with the genetic method for interpreting theological movements so firmly established, there is a temptation to linger at great lengths over the remote and the immediate background. To a degree, of course, this is absolutely necessary. Serious intellectual movements do not merely grow out of what went before, and then leave it, as it were, behind. Rather, the language of such movements retains history as an indispensable key to current meaning. For if dictionary definitions could be given to the pivotal words and formulas, the definitions would run, not a few lines, but several chapters; and it is history that would have written those chapters.

On the other hand, the role of history can also be exaggerated, and at the expense of an equally scientific examination into the present. We see this in the tendency to read what is being said today as too much of a simple repetition, or only slightly modernized variation, of what was being said yesterday. In point of fact, however, there is a job that history (in the usual sense) cannot do, and must therefore give way to a methodology that, while still conscious of history and of the past, attempts to engage also, and with equal seriousness, the immediate. History, in other words, yields only a part of the total meaning of the immediate. This is because history as an interpretative science comes up to the present and stops short; the present itself is insufficiently settled for the tools of historical digging. The bonafide historian senses this, and accepts the natural limitations of his discipline. But the historical extremist tries to get around the difficulty by simply pushing the present back into the past: "it has all been said before."

The point is particularly relevant to the Secularization movement. In our view, not a single personality linked to this movement could be said, in the accepted use of the academic expression, to belong to this or that "school." Van Buren comes closest. He identifies himself as a linguistic analyst and follower of the contemporary British school. But does he? As will be seen later, van Buren's position is rather that of an independent thinker who has discovered among certain British linguistic analysts a trend of thought that is quite sympathetic to his own, and has proved of some assistance in supplying a vehicle for the more systematic articulation of what he keeps referring to, in refreshingly unsophisticated terms, as his basic personal "attitudes." Robinson, for his part, does look consistently in a single direction, but the view covers enormous ground, and in the final analysis Robinson is almost uproariously eclectic. Moreover, as we suggested earlier, Robinson shows many signs of being a man of a number of ideas and hunches that are strictly, and in a sense initiatively, his own, but who wants to give credit to those who performed the landscaping in which his own sentiments are

most at home—except for the extent to which he attaches more directly to Bonhoeffer. Finally, Cox may be described as a sociological theologian, or something to that effect. But if the designation is to mean a school, and not merely an avocation, the school in question would be, again, very much his own.

In summary, then, Secularization's message is really its own. In one respect, it draws, as we have seen, from several sources, many of which, and perhaps the most important of which, history, theological history specifically, is ill-equipped to handle. Not only is the ground insufficiently settled, it is not normally recognized as theological ground to begin with. In another and far more significant respect, however, Secularization's message is an attempt to give articulate utterance to a vast religious phenomenon which is taking place in our times, but whose religious quality is being almost totally missed, thus leaving the phenomenon without the benefit of scientifically theological guidance.

Instead, however, of stating immediately the main elements of the message as they appear after a careful straining process, it will be useful to approach the matter a bit more gradually, and begin by asking the questions that will undoubtedly occur right away to the man on the street. For the man on the street, and the fault lies rather with the advertising than with his own lack of perception, the Secularization movement is all mixed up with *Death of God,* and like the latter, seems to be at one and the same time both atheist and Christian. At least that is what the double claim seems to be. Let us pose, then, these two lead questions: Is Secularization really atheist? Is it really Christian?

It goes without saying that just to frame the lead questions that way is a little odd. One would not be surprised to hear someone ask, first, whether a thing was theist, and then, anticipating an affirmative reply to this first question, whether it was

not only theist but also Christian. Nor, negatively, would anyone be surprised to hear someone ask, first, whether a thing was non-Christian, and then, again anticipating an affirmative reply to this first question, whether it was not only non-Christian but also non-theist or atheist. On the other hand, to pose first not the question of theism but the question of the atheistic denial, and then still go on even to raise the question of Christianity, is unusual. The procedure, nevertheless, is appropriate. In Secularization, and still more in *Death of God* from which Secularization is insufficiently distinguished, the possibility of atheism has at least to be considered. The very name *Death of God* would seem actually to proclaim that *Death of God* was atheist, and the name Secularization, if not in its own right, then certainly by reason of the popular confusion with *Death of God,* at least suggests it. Strangely, however, the fact that even the most radical forms of Secularization are Christian, want to be Christian, is a good deal more certain than the possibility, some would say very strong possibility, that they are also atheist. This is also true of *Death of God.*

With Bultmann, the question could have been: What happens to Christ? With Secularization—in its radical forms, and even in some of its more moderate forms—the question becomes: What happens to God?

This does not mean, however, that the newer movement simply goes "one step further." The matter is rather more complicated. On the one hand, the newer movement wants to extend some sort of theological reassessment all the way to the word "God," whereas Bultmann's demythologizing had taken in the angelic messengers, the voices from heaven, even a miraculous conception and the incarnation of a divine person, but had not touched "God." But if the newer movement touches *more* than Bultmann, it touches *everything* in a different way. With Bultmann, what was demythologized could no longer be taken literally, or at face value. The miracles, the apparitions, even

the miraculous birth and the incarnation were not such "in objective reality." Nor are they such in objective reality for van Buren. Nor, for van Buren, is God; or more accurately, one cannot say yes or no to the question, and must therefore keep silence. Put this way, there is an obvious but perhaps superficial sense in which at least van Buren goes one step further than Bultmann. But the same cannot be said of either Robinson or Cox. For neither Robinson nor Cox do the incarnation and divinity of Jesus cease to be such in objective reality. As we shall see, both not only confess the divinity of Christ, but even accept the unequivocal dogmatic formulations of divinity by Nicaea and Chalcedon. In this sense, therefore, Robinson and Cox do not go "further" than Bultmann, but not "so far." And if in another sense they nevertheless attempt, unlike Bultmann, to do something even with God, this something is not really a case of Bultmannian demythologizing. What it is, is an attempt to put God, without demythologizing him or "reducing" him, back on earth: to make the transcendent totally immanent without ceasing to affirm God's objective reality. At least this is the intention.

Before examining that intention more closely, however, and extending the test for occult atheism, we should observe that on still another point Secularization, as compared with Bultmann, can be said to go not "so far." This is the importance and unique centrality which it assigns to the "this-world" Jesus of Nazareth. Van Buren is explicit in this regard in his criticism of Bultmann and Ogden. In contrast to Bultmann, in fact, van Buren the radical speaks here as the conservative who is bringing Christ and historicity back, though again it is strictly a this-world Christ.

It remains, however, that Secularization, following out Bonhoeffer's suggestion as to what had been lacking in Bultmann, raises somewhat the same question about God himself that Bultmann raised about the supranatural projections. We must persist in asking, therefore: In the radical Secularization, does God really "go"? Is the movement ultimately atheist?

The first thing to look for would be simple statements saying either yes or no. But for very good reasons, we will not find either. Neither Robinson nor Cox nor even van Buren says, or even wants to say, that there is no God. No one of them denies the existence of God. Yet at the same time, no one of them wants to make, without at least some qualification, a simple reaffirmation of traditional theistic faith. One must look further, then, to discover whether the demur touches or not the substance of that faith.

Robinson, in one moment of his oscillation, is at least tempted to deny the existence of a God who is transcendent. There is no God "up there" or "out there" at all. But the temptation would be atheist only if the God brought back to earth, into the depth of the human situation and man's ultimate concern, were so immanentized as to lose all objective and distinct reality. Yet, Robinson does not want to talk in these terms. When all is said and done, however, Robinson's serious remarks do not seem to affect any other God than the one who has been projected into space by religious imagination, or projected into a sort of spiritual space by the classical metaphysics he takes to be just as naive. For Tillich was absolutely right: God cannot possibly be *a* being. (But on this last point, as Mascall is quick to observe, to Tillich and Robinson we would have to add Thomas Aquinas.)

In an essay now contained in the David Edwards collection entitled *The Honest to God Debate,* Alasdair MacIntyre began with a rather alarming first sentence: "What is striking about Dr. Robinson's book is first and foremost that he is an atheist." Mascall, however, himself no gentle prosecutor as a rule, sees no solid basis for pressing such a charge. In his style of speaking, the bishop seems to waver between belief and unbelief, and Mascall does fault the irresponsibility of the style. On closer inspection, nevertheless, the wavering is between a desire now to retain, now to abdicate, not God, but the traditional way of speaking about him.

John Robinson, then, believes in God, and in his subsequent work entitled with a question mark *The New Reformation?* he expresses much more incisively his "act of faith": Jesus is Lord and Son of the Father. Nor is there any serious question in Robinson's writings of an atheism occult and unsuspected. If at one minute he attempts to make totally immanent the transcendent being, at another he does not fail to repeat that the transcendent being exists and continues to be transcendent.

There is, however, a difficulty in all this, even if not of atheism precisely. It could be said, perhaps, that Robinson has called attention to what might be called the practical problems with belief in transcendent being, though in our judgment this would not hold a candle to the more socio-pastoral and ascetical service he had performed by attempting to develop positively the Bonhoeffer theme of "the man for others." But it could not be said, still in our judgment, and for all that Robinson has contributed much along several other lines, that he has contributed anything to the solution of the transcendence problem in particular. In fact, the way he keeps harping on a total immanentization of the transcendent, constantly repeating the notion without expanding upon it, makes it sound like an attempt to achieve a *pictorial* fusion of the Creator with finite being. But man cannot form even a proper and immediate concept, let alone picture, of transcendent being. The most he can do is judge that transcendent being exists, and that otherwise finite being would be meaningless. This particular plea of Robinson's, therefore, puts us back where we started: with a God who is pictured and imagined. The God seen somehow to melt with the finite is ultimately just as much of an imaginative projection as the God "up there" or "out there" that Robinson is so anxious to remove.

Then too, there is something here of having the cake and

eating it. We all know that Robinson positively hates the very name of metaphysics, and that is his privilege. And if in his later book *The New Reformation?* he makes clearer his act of faith in the God of Christian revelation, in the same volume and right in the same section he likewise makes more clear his violent "un-faith" in metaphysics. But it is Robinson himself who raises the metaphysical question of transcendence and immanence, not some challenger. And he raises it only to walk away from it. All he gives us is the otherwise unstructured and unexplained parallelism: the transcendent exists, and exists as transcendent; the transcendent exists, and exists as totally immanent. But yes or no, is God then objectively other? Once more, however, Robinson does not really want to talk in this language. "There you go with metaphysics again!" seems to be his exit line.

Harvey Cox shares completely Robinson's dissatisfaction with the God of traditional Christian theism. But it turns out to be the hellenized God of Plato and Aristotle. And Cox more than shares Robinson's antipathy for metaphysics. Cox, too, therefore, wants to put God, the strictly biblical God, back on earth.

On the other hand, again like Robinson, and as already remarked, Cox accepts not only the divinity of Christ, but the divinity of Christ precisely in its Nicene and Chalcedonian formulations. And in one of his final paragraphs in *The Secular City,* he makes his own theism as clear as one could wish. "We cannot simply conjure up a new name. Nor can we arbitrarily discard the old one. God does reveal his name in history, through the clash of historical forces and the faithful efforts of a people to discern His presence and respond to His call. A new name will come when God is ready. A new way of conceptualizing the Other will emerge in the tension between the history which has gone before us and the events which lie ahead. It will emerge as the issues of the urban civilization are drawn into that rehearsal of the past, reflection on the present, and responsibility for the future which *is* history." And Cox goes on to discuss the possibility that in the meantime we may have to "take a moratorium on speech" and stop talking about "God" "for a while." To borrow the punctuational code which the new radical theologians love so much, we can say, therefore, that for Cox there is no problem with God, but only with "God." More recently, in a review of Leslie Dewart's *The Future of Belief* which appeared in the book supplement of *Herder Correspondence* for September, 1966, Cox reflects his own basic stance in what he says of the *Death of God* theologians: "They are concerned to publish the word of the death of the God of Christian theism. But the God they inter is precisely the hellenized *theos* we have inherited from the hellenic phase of Christian history." And he goes on to show how in a sense Dewart actually goes further.

In its own fashion, then, Cox's moratorium and the expectancy of a new revelation in history may sound far out. But Cox certainly believes in God. Yet, as with Robinson, there remains a difficulty: the ultimate implications of Cox's "historical immanentism" and what becomes in this view of the uniquely privileged quality that attaches to the Judaeo-Christian revelation. We must transmit this consideration, however, to what will be its more natural place in the course of our third chapter.

Paul van Buren, in contrast to Robinson and Cox, does present a problem. Mascall, for instance, states quite categorically that van Buren "does not believe in God, [though] he does very sincerely believe in Jesus."

The matter comes to a point (to as much of a point as van Buren will let it) in the clear, swiftly paced opening chapters and sub-chapters of Part Two in *The Secular Meaning of the Gospel.* Having outlined the problem and explained his method, van Buren here gets on to his main task of coming to terms with the Gospel language. He begins with a consideration of "the historical Jesus," observing, and rightly, that Christianity simply has no other base. Before the disciples could "see" Jesus in a new way, through the Easter experience, they had first, obviously, to have seen him and known him in an old way, an ordinary way. And this is no less true of ourselves, and our need of "contact," through the New Testament witness, with the same historical Jesus. In addition to the confession "Jesus is Lord," and as the same confession's indispensable presupposition, we need the vicarious seeing him and knowing him that is given to us in the "historical" element of the Gospel.

On the other hand, van Buren continues immediately, there were no Christians before Easter. Whatever Easter was, whatever happened, Easter was decisive. What, then, *did* happen? What *was* Easter? For van Buren Easter was something, first of all, unquestionably real. It was at least an experience which the disciples actually had. It is meaningless, moreover, to ask if this Easter-experience was a merely subjective experience. For "every experience is subjective, by definition. . . . An experience, however, is always an experience of something, also by definition. The experience of Peter and the others on Easter was [therefore] certainly their own 'subjective' experience. But it was an experience of Jesus and his freedom in a way which was quite new for them. They may still have been attracted by their memory of Jesus. But on Easter they found themselves beginning to share in this freedom, and this had not happened to them before."

In the preceding paragraph, van Buren had given a neat summary of what was, in his interpretation, the content of the Easter experience. "Easter faith was a new perspective upon life arising out of a situation of discernment focussed on the history of Jesus. The peculiar relationship of this discernment to that history was determined by the peculiar experience which the disciples had on Easter. This was an experience of seeing Jesus in a *new* way and sharing in the freedom which had been his. One might convey better the tone of the disciples' words if one said that on Easter they found that Jesus had a new power which he had not had, or had not exercised, before: the power to awaken freedom also in them. Bonhoeffer's words are suggestive in this connection: 'The experience of transcendence is Jesus' being-for-others. His omnipotence, omniscience and omnipresence arise solely out of his freedom from self, out of his freedom to be for the others even unto death'. What happened to the disciples on Easter was that they came to share in this freedom to be for the others."

Now traditional Christianity would have no necessary or automatic quarrel with van Buren's interpretation so far as it goes. As a description of the impact of Easter upon the disciples, it is not only enlightening, but expressed in terms of very pointed contemporary relevance. Traditional Christianity, however, is going to ask after what the interpretation fails to mention. But what about the resurrection itself?

Yet, the more truly serious question here, and the one van Buren himself is candid enough to recognize as such, is that of divinity. What about *God?* Is the one newly "seen," whose freedom is now, as van Buren puts it, caught by contagion, the risen *Lord* Jesus? For the resurrection, the bodily resurrection, certainly includes in its full meaning the continued, distinct life of the *Lord* Jesus Christ. This confession of the lordship of Jesus was the very essence of the most ancient Christian credal formulas eventually woven into the texture of the New Testament.

But van Buren actually admits this. Having passed from the historical Jesus of Nazareth to the Easter event, he moves on without interruption to the confession of the primitive community: "Jesus is Lord." For "Jesus is Lord" was simply their way of saying, and witnessing to, the resurrection. Van Buren moreover, is perfectly aware of the divinity implication—or if the word "divinity" causes special difficulties, of the God implication—in this resurrection witness. His manner of speaking at this juncture is consequently of extreme importance. What it amounts to, in fact, is a most conscious and deliberate insistence on stopping short of divinity, or God, in determining, as a theological empiricist, what the resurrection confession really, logically, simply has to mean. "Those who first said, 'Jesus is Lord', expressed a particular perspective upon life and history. This confession, ascribing universality to a particular man, indicated that faith constituted a certain understanding of self, man, history, and the whole world, and that this universal perspective had its norm in the history of Jesus of Nazareth and Easter."

As the reader may want to note, stopping short of affirming something is not the same thing as denying it. Will van Buren, then, ever declare himself on the reality of God? Yes, actually he will, and right at the end of his discussion of the Easter confession. He realizes that he has raised the question himself, and that taking a stand cannot be further postponed. The stand he takes, however, is neither affirmation or denial, but silence. He avails himself of a suggestion made by one of the linguistic analysts, T. R. Miles. "Miles has spoken of faith as the way of silence qualified by parables. Certainly the Christian possesses no special sources for the scientific description of the universe. Before such questions as to whether there is some absolute being, even 'Being itself', which is 'behind' or 'beyond' all we know and are, some final 'ground and end of all created things', he will be wise to remain silent. He may qualify his silence, however, by telling something beside a parable. What he has to tell is the history of Jesus and the strange story of how his freedom became contagious on Easter."

As our own discussion continues, an attempt will be made to confront this silence on its declared terms. Many "answers" could be suggested: exegetical, theological, philosophical. But in our judgment, they would not meet van Buren's precise challenge. For what actually stands behind and supports van Buren's rigidly empiricist reductionism, as also his insistent silence, is an ideal of secularist responsibility. Confrontation can, and to be effective must, assume the same stance. Is silence at this point really responsible? Even in the strictly secularist sense?

We shall return, then, to the deeper aspect of van Buren's option for silence. The reader should observe, however, that it is at least not a flat denial. Further, he should note the context. On the one hand, van Buren does generalize. In the passage just cited, he speaks of "the Christian," and says of him that "he will be wise to remain silent." This is to go quite beyond a statement that might have read: "As to the question of God's reality, I would prefer not to take up that question in the course of this particular study." On the other hand, van Buren is concerned throughout this particular study, not with God, but with "God" —the word, the piece of language. In his favor, so to speak, is the fact that "God" is a word. Also in his favor, is the fact that God is not an *empirical* reality, exactly as van Buren says he is not. Against him, on the other hand, is his assumption, when all is said and done, that the only serious use of language is to name empirical reality, or at least to function in the over-all setting and context of empirical reality, as in the use of language to proclaim a basic attitude, or *blik,* or new perspective. Even here, he has a point. This is at least the first use of language; and it remains in some sense paradigmatic in every other and further use. Nevertheless, language is *de facto* used, today as at any other time, for what is non-empirical, and when it is so used it is used seriously. Thus, van Buren is certainly correct in observing that modern man is empirically minded. He asks rather too much of us, however, when he wants to add: exclusively so. Not even his fellow radicals will grant him this. From the *Death of God* side, Altizer, in *Mircea Eliade and the Dialectic of the Sacred,* takes quite a strong stand against this particular type of secularist mentality and appeals with Rudolf Otto for a rediscovery of the transcendent sacred. And Cox is actually explicit: towards the end of *The Secular City,* he points to van Buren by name and challenges precisely this pan-empiricist assumption.

The second question—Is Secularization a specifically *Christian* movement?—is, as we remarked above, easier to answer. Curiously, it is especially easier to answer, and affirmatively, in the case of van Buren.

For traditional Christianity, of course, the ultimate yes or no here hinges upon acknowledgement of Christ's true divinity. In the traditionalist eye, therefore, van Buren could be called a "Christian" only in a wider sense. In the same traditionalist eye, however, countless other Christians are "Christians" only in a wider sense. But in the contemporary religious and theological dialogue, italics or quotation marks are dropped. The man who is a Christian in his own professed intention is at least allowed the name. And this is as it should be.

Van Buren's intention is quite clear. *The Secular Meaning of the Gospel* is meant to be, in fact, a Christology. What might be called the sincerity of van Buren's stance is especially well brought out, as we have already seen, in his criticism of Bultmann on historicity, and his own insistence upon the undiminished role of *Jesus historicus*. It is likewise brought out, again as we have seen, in precisely those passages where the question of van Buren's belief in God becomes both critical and explicit.

Honest to God, too, and at least in its intention, is a specifically Christian manifesto. Its predominant theme, and this is carried over into *The New Reformation?*, is that of the Bonhoeffer "man for others." Nor does Robinson have any real problem with divinity. His problem, particularly in the *Honest to God* chapter entitled "The Man for Others," is rather with following the way of Hellenism, as he considers it to be, into the static and lifeless Christ of Chalcedonian God-manhood, thus leaving behind and unknown the New Testament man for others. But as Robinson himself adds, even if with mixed enthusiasm, "the naturalist interpretation of Christ [does not] side with Athanasius on what he recognized to be the crucial divide. To say that Jesus had a unique experience of God, that he was

like God or that God was like him—this can never add up to
saying that he was 'of one substance' with the Father. And on
that line Athanasius was correct in seeing that the battle must
be fought, however much one may legitimately deplore the
categories in which that test of orthodoxy had to be framed."
Put that way, Robinson's position on hellenization is hardly
radical. It is shared, for instance, by so conservative a theologian
as Oscar Cullmann, whose remarks (though in a subsequent
article he was to qualify them a bit further) in the introduction
to his *Christology of the New Testament* are an almost verbal
anticipation of what we have just quoted from *Honest to God.*

As for Cox, the Christianity and Christocentricism of *The
Secular City* may be slightly more problematical. First, in the
key chapter entitled "Toward a Theology of Social Change"
Cox, too, raises the matter of Chalcedon and God-manhood. His
sentiments, though much more briefly expressed, seem in the
main to be the same as Robinson's. Cox does not reject the
doctrine of Chalcedon: rather, he takes its legitimacy for
granted, and simply calls for contemporary reinterpretation.

Also, despite superficial impressions that certain of his remarks might occasion, Cox's plea for total secularization does
not really attack Christianity. When he states, as he does so frequently, that Christendom is a thing of the past, he means what
Christendom became in shape and style through the long centuries of its evolving. Further, as Cox urges apropos of the
"pragmatism" of John F. Kennedy and the "profanity" of Albert
Camus, there is no essential opposition between the secular ideal,
on the one hand, and the biblical and Gospel ideal, on the
other. Rather, secularization has its roots in the authentic message of the Judaeo-Christian liberation.

Biblical theologians, and Old Testament scholars particularly,
may experience some discomfort at the extraordinarily neat, and
in any case onesided, exegesis which Cox offers of the Pentateuch
to prove the point last mentioned. Also, as Mascall has noted in

the case of Robinson, there comes a time when the historians of both conciliar and medieval theology have to call attention to the degree of oversimplification in much of the present-day diatribe against Hellenism and its metaphysics. When both Robinson and Cox talk about the metaphysical mentality and the metaphysical stage of development, they give evidence, unfortunately, of only having been acquainted with metaphysics at its absolutely worst: there metaphysics degenerates into talk about talk, an endless game of neat concepts and instant universes, rather than an effort of critical understanding. In this regard, Leslie Dewart's *The Future of Belief,* a more recent contribution to the new radical theology, comes off much better. When Dewart argues that we have not yet appropriated the ultimate significance of the hellenization phenomenon and its metaphysical tradition, he does so at least as an insider, and this gives his criticism of metaphysics a more seriously thought-provoking sting.

To return to the subject at hand, however, Cox's *The Secular City* is certainly in a broad sense a Christian statement. Is it, however, a conscious and deliberate Christology as is van Buren's *The Secular Meaning of the Gospel?* Is it as blatantly Christocentric as Robinson's *Honest to God?* If one looks in *The Secular City* for the expansion of a Christological theme, a theme in which the person and identity of Christ would be the immediate point of discussion and constant preoccupation, the reply to both of these questions will probably have to be no. But this could be deceiving. On the one hand, Cox mentions occasionally, but does not develop, the Bonhoeffer emphasis on "the man for others." On the other hand, however, the entire book attempts to define the spiritual perspective, and even blueprint the career, of precisely the individual in the secular city who has made "the man for others"—the Bonhoeffer Christ, therefore—his unique ideal. In our opinion, the creative spirit of *The Secular City* is not only Christological, but profoundly so, in essence.

The Secularization movement, then, is not at all a plea for positive atheism. Even van Buren replies, equivalently, to his challenger: "You ask me if I believe in God as an objective reality; I can only answer that I do not know what that would logically have to mean." Nor, secondly, does the movement constitute an attack upon Christianity, or seek simply to displace Christianity—for all that it may, and does, attack certain forms of Christianity. The settlement of these two initial questions is vital to any attempt at meaningful and effective confrontation. For on the surface, the movement could appear to be little more than a present-day reassertion of oldfashioned scientific rationalism. Admittedly, there is a strong rationalist flavor in its motivation, but there is totally lacking the well-known sometime rationalist dismissal of Christianity as a subject worthy of the serious conversation of intelligent people. In fact, the presupposition of the movement is precisely the opposite.

Up to now, however, we have been concerned, and quite necessarily, with what Secularization is not: neither positive atheism, nor an attack upon Christianity as such. For the remainder of this chapter, we shall be concerned, then, with what it is. Of course, we have already established one positive point in the course of replying to the question whether or not Secularization is specifically Christian: in general, it is not merely Christian, at least in its avowed intention, but even consciously Christocentric, meaning that, faithful to the main thrust of Bonhoeffer's theology, it sees the entirety of Christian existence as formal assimilation to "the man for others."

But to continue, what Secularization wants to do is (1) to rid Christianity of its "other-worldliness" (at least in some sense), and (2) thereby make Christianity a "this-worldly" creative force. The second of these two objectives is, to be sure, quite inseparable from the Christocentricist principle already discovered. For what the "this-worldly" creative force had in mind is that which is achieved as the whole Christian community becomes "the man for others."

There is, then, a negative element. Something very definitely has to go. But that something is clearly not Christianity. And it is not, so to speak, even God: unless it be the "other-worldly God," and this latter understood as a projection of religious symbolism. As we have observed, Robinson believes in God; nevertheless, he wants to banish the "other-worldly," even the "other-worldly God." Cox believes in God; but Cox also wants to have done with the "other-worldly," even, in his case too, the "other-worldly God." Van Buren, on the other hand, does not profess belief in God. He opts for silence; but the precise reason for his silence is that he cannot any longer talk about the "other-worldly," including the "other-worldly God."

The reader may wonder at this point whether "other-worldly" is merely the modernized version of what classical theology calls *supernatural*. Actually, no. "Other-worldly" as used in the contemporary radical dialogue extends to a great deal more than what classical theology calls the *supernatural*—and at the same time, to a great deal less.

First, then, for the more. Classical theology makes a triple division. It speaks of the *divine,* which is simply God. It speaks of the *supernatural,* which is not divine substantially, but something created and finite: the whole order of grace whereby man is brought in some ineffable way to share in God's own life, and to do so utterly beyond the capacities of his merely human *nature*—and so the word: *super-nature.* Finally, it speaks of the *preternatural,* which is more or less equivalent, at least for our immediate purposes, to the *miraculous.* But for all of these categories, and for still further subdivisions and combinations which we have not mentioned, the new radical theology speaks simply of the "other-worldly," and uses terms like "*supernatural*" and "*supranatural*" as substitutes for "other-worldly." God, or more accurately "God" (the "God" in heaven up above) is thus "other-worldly." The life hereafter is clearly "other-worldly." The virgin birth of the Son of God is also "other-worldly."

But now for the less. If "other-worldly" is the broadest of theological formulas in its extension, it is one of the shortest in its penetration. It is meant to include miracles and apparitions, revelations and divine interventions, the life of grace and the very being of God; but it is simultaneously meant to pierce any and every one of these only to the level of speech and concept. The traditional Christian theologian, once he sees what is going on here, will attempt to clear the air: "Fine. I read you clearly. You're talking about all these things at the level of religious symbolism. But will you now answer my question; What is your position about these same things at the level of objective reality?" And here is the impasse. The radical theologian will either refuse to say anything whatsoever, pro or con, at the so-called level of objective reality (van Buren), or commit himself briefly, and so far as the traditionalist is concerned even satisfactorily, but nevertheless refuse at least to integrate his stand on the objective realities into his socio-religious program for revitalized Christianity (Robinson and Cox). The traditionalist may feel exasperated, therefore, but he should find some consolation in the fact that if everything is falling down it is not falling from much of a distance.

In any case, for the Secularization theologians as a group everything "other-worldly" has at least in some sense to be brought back to earth—the implication being that that is where it started from in the process of symbolic projection. In his *The Secularization of Christianity,* referring to Robinson, Van Buren, and other authors who exhibit the same tendencies, Mascall calls this bringing of the "other-worldly" back to earth "reductionism." Van Buren himself had actually used the expression in his *The Secular Meaning of the Gospel.* And as we noted earlier, the new radical reductionism does represent certain basic features of

Bultmann's demythologizing. But we also noted significant points of difference. Bultmann had not, as it were, touched God, and this is where Bonhoeffer had found him at fault. Bultmann's concern had been rather with the talk *about* God—his activity in the world of men, etc.—beginning with the talk *about* God in Sacred Scripture. His intention had been to get behind the no longer sense-making and relevant mythology, in which the biblical account of God and man's dependence upon him was expressed, in order that the essential and timeless message might be exposed and reinterpreted. Van Buren and Robinson, however, following Bonhoeffer's original suggestion, want to get right to the secular bottom of religious language as such, and reinterpret God—or better, "God." God, moreover, or "God," is not strictly speaking demythologized, but secularized. In a very important sense, he is left intact even while becoming secularized. Thus, Robinson, for example, can both insist upon bringing him back to earth, and nevertheless continue, as we have observed, almost in the same breath to accept the Nicene definition of Christ's true divinity. Bultmann could never have done that.

At this juncture, the reader might feel tantalized and wonder if the question of atheism is not automatically brought up all over again. If Secularization comes to terms, not with the talk *about* him, but with God himself, how can atheism, at least an "on again–off again" atheism, possibly be avoided? We can only repeat, however, that if the new radical theology seems to go beyond Bultmann in this respect, and come to terms even with God, it is not God really, but "God." "God" is God as spoken, God as named. That is how Robinson and Cox can both want to change "God," put "God" back on earth, at times even contemplate doing away with "God," and still accept Nicaea and Chalcedon. That is how even van Buren, who is not a believer in the accepted sense, can at least consider the question of the reality of God as a question distinct, and choose to maintain silence upon it while nevertheless positively getting rid of "God."

But *why* should anybody be so passionately bent on doing away with the "other-worldly" and its "God" in the first place? This is the question that brings us to the heart of the matter.

There is, first of all, the motive of intellectual honesty, of wanting to state, argue and pass on in serious discourse with one's contemporaries, what one simply believes to be both true in itself and crucial for the times. And if it can be said that any mature author operates on such a motive, it must be said with additional emphasis in the case of the secularizationists: intellectual honesty is simply a facet of that *responsibility,* which, particularly as it guides dedication to humanity, is the cardinal virtue of the Secularization movement.

Intellectual honesty, here the honesty of strictly objective scholarship, predominates in van Buren. Yet, a comment might be inserted. There was a time when the totally scientific quest for truth was qualified as disinterested. Today, however, disinterested does not appear to be quite the right word. Today, in fact, there is apt to be difficulty even with the word "objective." The scholar's quest continues to adhere to the ideal of objectivity and disinterestedness insofar as it is scientifically nonpartisan, utterly free from false absolutes and aprioris. But in recent years, the very same quest has come more and more to adhere as well to a second ideal, an ideal of a different order, and an ideal that in no way conflicts with the first, but rather supports the first with a new and deeper purposefulness. It is the ideal of *social* and *historical* responsibility. Thus, in van Buren it is not the clergyman that comes to the fore, but the theological scientist. His message, however, even as that of the theological scientist, is addressed as much to contemporary life as to Academe. In van Buren's mind, it is important that modern man rediscover and live the Christian Gospel—in its "secular meaning." But this calls for a process of purification. If the Christian Gospel is to be understood, and in its authentically secular meaning, it must be stripped of the "other-worldly."

Speaking of the present-day Christian, therefore, van Buren can write in his chapter on "The Meaning of the Gospel" that the Christian's "assertion, 'Jesus is Lord,' expresses the fact that Jesus has become his point of orientation, with the consequence that he is freed from acknowledging final loyalty to his nation, family, church, or any other person and is liberated for service to these other centers of relative loyalty. Because he sees not only his own history but the history of all men in the light of the one history of Jesus of Nazareth and Easter, he will not rest content when his nation, family, or church seek to live only for themselves; he will try to set them in the service of others." And so will van Buren. The Gospel of Jesus and Easter, he is telling us, must be purified of all "other-worldly" interpretation; but what ultimately gives purpose and direction to the process, is social, historical, and in van Buren's fashion strictly Christian, responsibility.

Secondly, however, there is the motive of a more formal pastoral concern, the motive which our world normally associates with the Christian clergyman in the pursuance of his particular avocation. In Robinson, it jumps off almost every page. Likewise in Cox, it shows conspicuously, though without the sound effects. And if what we might call the avocational motive is absent from van Buren, this has to be taken in the context of the observation made above.

The particular reason, then, why Robinson and Cox want to bring God back to earth is because here is precisely where they believe he is, and is to be found. If modern secular man is to know and serve any God at all, if he is to rediscover God and a spiritual life, it can only be the God in and of this world. That is why the churches must stop fighting secularization. For in a sense, they are fighting God. And that is why the "God up there," or the "God out there," or the "God" of "other-worldliness," has to go. "His" presence is but a continued obstacle to the discovery of God *in* the secular city.

This does not mean that Robinson and Cox are saying entirely the same thing. Robinson, for example, offers us no socio-cultural, intentionally scientific, analysis of urbanization and *de facto* secularization, the way Cox does. True, in *The New Reformation?* Robinson, as it were, gets closer to Cox, particularly when he develops his "start at both ends" theme. Instead of working exclusively from the side of God and traditional theology, Robinson argues at this point, equivalently, that we begin and for a time stick with the secular, and do so in an effort to force into articulation the sacred and the spiritual—and the authentically Christian—that in a sense is already there. The, we might call it "inductivism," of such an approach, as opposed to the rigidly "deductivist" approach which has been more traditional, very definitely reminds one of Cox. On the other hand, and very much unlike Cox, Robinson still employs the "two worlds" idiom in suggesting what should be the basic attitude of today's clergyman. Hence, there remains a sort of integration through confrontation, rather than a simple discovery of the secular-religious, or secular-spiritual, *one,* however, nebulous that one may presently be. In point of fact, when delivering the lectures that eventually became *The New Reformation?,* Robinson would not have been able to consult *The Secular City,* as the latter had not yet appeared. And even when, at the time of publication, Robinson was revising these lectures, he was able only to consult the manuscript version, which he mentions in a footnote, and that only after having completed his own text. Thus far, therefore, Robinson merely draws our attention, in the manner of an educated observer, to the more or less indisputable qualities of our age as the existential climate for the new reform. Much less does Robinson invite us to examine the virtues that Cox, on the other hand, finds growing naturally, spontaneously, out of the "shape" and "style" of secularization. Someone could say to Robinson, in fact, and with Cox in mind, "You keep telling me to read the book of this world, but you don't tell me *how*."

Robinson, in any event, takes for granted the worldliness of the world, and the chasm that consequently separates the world from the Gospel of Jesus and from God. He wants to close, if he can, the gap—to make faith, if not easy, at least possible. If he has not Cox's insight to spot good where religion up to now has at least suspected nothing but evil—the basic "shape" and "style" of technopolis—he will at least pursue, and extend, the Bultmannian program of purging religion from everything that modern, secular man finds intolerable. He will attempt to strip the traditional Christian message from whatever the man of the world cannot even begin to accept. *And,* the bishop adds, there is no valid reason why he should have to accept it in the first place. It is not, and never was, essential to the Gospel message. What concretely does Robinson have in mind? Two things: the whole machinery of the "other-worldly" that is used to talk about Christianity's God, his revelation to man, and his over-all intervention in human affairs; plus whatever in Christianity's blueprint for behavior, or moral code, really belongs to, and depends upon, the same "other-worldly" perspectives.

Thus, through several long passages (long for a little book like *Honest to God*), Robinson pounds away at traditional Christianity's "triple-decker" universe. As Mascall observes, the bishop's opponent at this point in the debate is not traditional Christianity, but very nearly its caricature. Yet, we agree only partly with Mascall. Robinson's may not be a fair picture of what Christianity ever was, either at the level of official utterance and articulate theologizing, or at the level of simple but authentic faith. But the bishop has learned from personal experience, as have many others, that authentic Christian faith is not infrequently smudged with a good deal of downright magic, even today, and even among otherwise mature and educated people, the clergy by no means excepted. In any case, as we have seen already, for Robinson the God "up there" and the God "out there" simply has to go. In "his" stead, Robinson suggests the Tillichian notion of God as the ground and end of all created things. If the man of the world hotly refuses to stop thinking about the deepest problems of life, society, history, to interrupt his quest for the ultimate meaning of existence—all in order to turn his attention to an "old man in the sky" or any more sophisticated version of the same mirage—Robinson will tell him that he agrees with him wholeheartedly. And this is certainly a good beginning. Nor does Robinson really negate transcendence. Once again, the God he brings back to earth remains "other," a conclusion implicit in his explicit act of faith, and in his fundamental acceptance of Nicaea. It is just that Robinson does not want to stress this, nor at least at the *start* of his conversation with the man of the world even so much as mention it. Thus the apologetic worked out in *The New Reformation?* is strictly an invitation to identify with the man Jesus of Nazareth.

A progression, moreover, can be noted between *Honest to God* and *The New Refomation?*. In the earlier and more rambunctious work, the focus is brought down from the "otherworldly" and back to Jesus. Again, Robinson does not deny his divinity. But he does want to point out that incarnation and divinity are not the Gospel's own preoccupation. He would be more correct if he said rather that it was not the introductory first lesson in the Gospel pedagogy, nor, as a rule, the object of immediate concentration. Robinson, however, and especially in *Honest to God,* does not like to make distinctions. But he is right in arguing that Jesus is first presented as a man, "the man for others." To be "the man for others" was, in fact, his earthly career, and it was only in the context of that career, not somehow apart from it, that his unique relationship to God was communicated.

This, then, is where Robinson wants to linger, at the point

where his man of the world could be brought to see that his own highest and noblest ideal of human love, service to others, and dedication to the causes of humanity, is not a non-Christian, purely humanistic, alternative to the Gospel: it *is* the Gospel.

Yet, there may be an objection to all of this—as left in *Honest to God*—and not quite the kind Robinson seems to expect. He anticipates an objection from the traditionalist theologian. He realizes that his method of unresolved parallel statements—now one side, now the other, but never reconciliation or synthesis—is going to encounter the clarifications, qualifications and distinctions of the traditionalists. But there is something else in Robinson's appeal to "the man for others" that is going to encounter no less the clarifications, qualifications and distinctions of the scientific and secular humanist, the man of the world's most competent spokesman. Without any lack of gratitude for the bishop's extraordinary degree of sympathy and identification with the people, problems and ideals of this world, he is going to want to say, nevertheless, that he has heard much of it before, from others equally well intentioned. The bishop wants to clean up theology so that the man of the world could sit down and talk it over. But the scientific and secular humanist feels that he in turn has something to say to the theologian. It is not enough, in his eyes, that Robinson professes himself to be a man of this world, though that is certainly a help. The further question is, how much is he a man of this world? There is more to the world than its being here on earth. There is more to the world than its being here by itself, alone, left to its own devices, without God and without an interest in God. Does the bishop really understand the world as an insider? Does he really appreciate not only its more obvious characteristics, along with its more obvious problems, but the ultimate energizing form and creativeness of its science, its technology, its urbanization? To the secular humanist, the bishop's heart is in the right place, that is to say, here on earth. And he is moving in the right direction. For Robinson's Christ, like Bonhoeffer's, has at least begun to be *Jesus sociologicus*. Nevertheless, Robinson is moving in generalities, wordly generalities.

In *The New Reformation?*, however, Robinson partly answers such an objection. Here, his stress on a strictly *lay* theology is more incisive. No longer can it be said that he wants to clean up theology so that the man of the world could sit down and talk it over. Rather, now he is waiting for the man of the world at least to divide the initiative. The result will be the lay theology. On the other hand, the bishop's remarks in this third chapter certainly imply that in his own mind he himself is not as yet "doing" such theology, and that he has not yet been able to benefit from the secular humanist's assumption of true initiative.

This is precisely where Harvey Cox comes in in *The Secular City*. For Cox, there can be no dialogue between Christian theology and the secular city until the secular city has been defined —*from within*. The theologian, on his part, has to be introduced to the secular city, and by the secular city or its authentic spokesman. As yet, he does not really know the secular city. And the reason is simply that the secular city has not as yet expressed itself to the theologian in a language which the theologian could recognize. But this means that the secular humanist, on his part, and in an effort to communicate in such a language, has to be introduced to—of all things!—theology, that is to say, the theology of the secular city. To put it another way, the man of the world must discover his own theological dimension and give it utterance.

Without prompting from the theologian, however, it will not occur to the scientific and secular humanist to attempt the secularly *theological* definition of the secular city. On the other hand, if the definition is to be *secularly* theological, no one else but a scientific and secular humanist will be able to attempt it. He alone has the partners of analysis and the formulas. Cox, therefore, will try to assume the indicated double role. As a religious sociologist, he will speak in the character of a scientific and secular humanist. For, again, any adequate definition of the secular city cannot but be in its own terms. As a Christian theologian, he will also speak in the character of one professionally qualified to observe and study the theological, even the secularly theological. For it is the specifically theological definition that is at the moment required.

There is an unevenness about the composition and order of *The Secular City*. Part One is entitled "The Coming of the Secular City," its opening chapter "The Biblical Sources of Secularization." But this way of beginning, and despite the existence of an introduction outside Part One, may be misleading. It can give the impression that the book is not only a *historia mundi,* but one told from a decidedly tendentious point of view. Actually, the book is neither. The chapter on the biblical sources is retrospective, as though the author had first presented his analysis of the modern secularization phenomenon, and then went on to demonstrate that the historical roots of the phenomenon were as a matter of fact biblical.

The crucial movement of Cox's argument can be outlined as follows. We are living in a secular age: look around. This secular or secularization phenomenon is generally taken to be what is most in opposition to, and destructive of, the Christian spirituality of our times: listen to the pastors and the theologians. If, however, we study with greater scientific care the anatomy of secularization, we see it to be not only unopposed to Christianity, but in profound agreement with Christianity, and dedicated, despite superficial appearances to the contrary, to what is most truly authentic and basic in the Christian Gospel.

First, then, Cox has to define the "secularized." Quite obviously, he has in mind something more than sprawling steel mills, crowded highways and millions of people watching television rather than going to Church. Such things as these are

merely part of the initial glance. Cox must examine the phenomenon much more deeply. He does this by considering in the
second and third chapters of the same Part One both the *shape*
and the *style* of the secular city. The two words would not be
far in meaning from its "body" and its "spirit" respectively.

In *shape,* the secular city is marked by two external, but extremely significant and influential, characteristics: anonymity
and mobility. Cox notes the typical religious and especially existentialist bemoaning of modern, anonymous man, the faceless
and depersonalized number. But the true sociological opposite
to anonymous is intimate, not personal. Modern urban man's
"being anonymous to most people permits him to have a face
and a name for others." The only way he can possibly be intimate, as indeed he ought to be, with some is to remain anonymous to the rest. Of still greater importance, however, is that
anonymity is a facet of liberation, of the biblically grounded
freedom from law and social convention which allows a man
to select and choose in his personal relationships with maturity
and responsibility. Anonymity, therefore, is not spiritually ob-
structive, but spiritually creative.

Of mobility, Cox speaks with understandably greater caution.
The opportunities for swift and frequent movement from place
to place can actually foster a spirit antithetical to maturity and
responsibility. This happens. But it is neither automatic nor
necessary. For mobility too, as yet another facet in urban man's
liberation from cultural and social determinants, vastly increases
the possibilities for mature and responsible personal decision.
There is likewise the very important consideration that mobility
exercises an essential role, again a spiritually creative role, in
effecting otherwise hopelessly retarded social change.

In *style,* as Cox terms it, the secular city is marked by two
further and more significant characteristics, this time affecting
immediately not simply its outer form but its conscious psychology: pragmatism and profanity—"profaneness" would per-

haps be a better word. By the former, Cox does not mean the philosophical dogmatism sometimes given that name, and by the latter he does not mean vulgarity. The pragmatist, and Cox cites John F. Kennedy as a prime example, is interested in getting things done, specific things, and getting such things done as best he can here and now. Moreover, "to say that technopolitan man is pragmatic means that he is a kind of modern ascetic. He disciplines himself to give up certain things. He approaches problems by isolating them from irrelevant considerations, by bringing to bear the knowledge of different specialists, and by getting ready to grapple with a new series of problems when these have been provisionally solved. Life for him is a set of problems, not an unfathomable mystery. He brackets off the things that cannot be dealt with and deals with those that can. He wastes little time thinking about 'ultimate' or 'religious' questions. And he can live with highly provisional solutions." Such functional-mindedness, so long as it does not degenerate into mere operationalism, is not at all contrary to the spirit of the New Testament. For its concept of truth is the strictly biblical concept of the true as the dependable, and its basic motivation is once more that of personal, social and historical responsibility.

Profanity (or profaneness), as Cox employs the term, hardly more than makes explicit the radical "this-worldliness" of technopolitan pragmatism. Not surprisingly, therefore, it is the discussion of profanity that brings into a single unified view both the negative and positive aspects of Cox's position: reduction of the "other-worldly," but solely in order to make Christianity a "this-worldly" creative force. What he says referring to Albert Camus in this section is worded very strongly. "Camus," Cox writes, "knew that there is an essential contradiction between the traditional Christian doctrine of God and the full freedom and responsibility of man. He faced this contradiction in all its seriousness, and we must face it too." Yet, as Cox goes on to clarify in the very same sub-chapter, what he means by "the traditional doctrine of God" is not biblical Christianity in its primordial state, but rather what became of this in the course of time. Further, he lays particular stress upon the Old Testament idea that was behind the "naming of the animals" in Genesis. The point is simply that man himself is to *continue* God's work of creation. The freedom, the mature responsibility, the spiritual creativeness, which Cox has been trying to put into focus throughout this section (and throughout the book) is now formally linked to the creative mandate expressed in Genesis.

For Cox, then, the Secularization of Christianity is not only not harmful but positively good, not only good but necessary. The virtues of the secular city—anonymity, mobility; pragmatism; profaneness; improvization; personal, social and historical responsibility—do not run counter to the Gospel, but in precisely the same direction. They do so, moreover, rather more realistically than in "other-worldly" Christianity, and in two senses. First, they coincide better than much of what we hear in the Churches with what was primary, not fringe, in the New Testament ideal, the ideal of charity in identification with "the man for others." Secondly, in their effective creativity they can actually be tested, measured almost. But the virtues practiced in the context of the "other-worldly" cannot.

Secularization, then, is by no means merely a tearing-down process. Even in van Buren, there is an element of religious constructiveness, far more in Robinson, and very much more in Cox.

The reductionism scored by Mascall remains, however. And it must be engaged in theological confrontation. If a valid point has been made, does it really carry along with itself, and as necessities, all of the corrollary "therefores"? The positive and creative message of a "this-worldly" Christian spirituality must also be discussed. Do its at least putative insights really grow out of the biblical dialogue and a new way of reading the New Testament, or from rather a different source altogether? Are they not, in a broad sense of the word, philosophical and evolutionist? And what becomes in such a view of the uniquely privileged quality that attaches to God's own self-disclosure in the Judaeo-Christian revelation, and in particular in his Christ? The question of death also arises, this time not the death of God, but the death of man. Can there be a 100 per cent "this-worldly" approach to what is still man's, even technopolitan man's, in many respects most basic problem of life—death?

Thus far, therefore, our presentation of the message is, to say the least, incomplete. A number of questions have yet to be posed and discussed. And until they are discussed, it will not be possible to attempt an answer to the final question: Where does Secularization appear to be going?

II.

The Break From Tradition

A. The Gospel and Historical Factuality

IN HIS BOOK *The Secularization of Christianity,* Eric Mascall devotes the fifth and final chapter, entitled "Fact and the Gospels," to the age-old problem of historic factuality in the Gospel accounts. The discussion covers a neat one-quarter of the entire work. But this is a bit misleading. In our judgment, what Secularization has to say about such matters as the corporal resurrection or the miraculous conception, the two crucial instances which Mascall singles out, is not in any true sense what is distinctive of the movement, or indeed of the whole new radical theology. Hence, it should not be given so much space. On the other hand, Mascall's focus actually turns out to be upon strictly present-day reductionist exegesis, and he extends his critique at this point to include not only van Buren and Robinson, but also, as a third major reductionist, John Knox. And admittedly, Knox's *The Church and the Reality of Christ* is very much preoccupied with the question of fact and Gospel. It is a scholarly, quietly provocative attempt of a well-known biblical theologian, writing precisely as a biblical theologian, to find in a highly specialized concept of the Church a fresh approach to the perennial difficulties.

Nevertheless, we do not want to extend our own investigation in similar fashion. In the first place, there is more to the Secularization movement than reductionist exegesis, and this would seem to be the real weakness in Mascall's albeit brilliant critique. Further, what reductionist exegesis Secularization does practise, differs significantly from that of either the Bultmannians or Knox. When all is said and done, Secularization assumes neither the style nor the method of a biblical theology in the stricter sense.

Our consideration of the movement's reductionism in what we might call the area of the Gospel mysteries, therefore, will be much more brief than Mascall's. In this same area, Secularization's "contribution" to reductionist exegesis might be summed up in one word: simplification. For what now has to go, as we have already noted, is simply the "other-worldly"—*everything* "other-worldly," not merely the miracles and the interventions. We must repeat, however, the element of paradox here: if the newer reductionism, as compared with the Bultmannian, reaches now to everything, God himself included, it penetrates less deeply. Bultmann's apparition was frankly deprived in the process of reinterpretation of all objective reference; but the God of Robinson and Cox, and in a way even van Buren, is not. For in the newer radical theology it is "God," not God, that is in question.

Thus, for van Buren, even the reality of God as objective and distinct is a matter upon which we can do no more than maintain a rigid silence. The resurrection, therefore, is interpreted not only without any reference to the divinity of Jesus, but with a deliberate and painstaking attempt to preclude such a reference. Robinson and Cox, on the other hand, do acknowledge both the reality of God and the divinity of Jesus. But they do not want to talk much about either, for this would be to return the conversation to the forbidden theme of the "other-worldly."

In any case, when it comes precisely to the physical resurrection and the virginal conception, the basic simplifying stance against the total "other-worldly" is preserved intact. Mascall notes that van Buren, Robinson, he adds Knox, differ in attitude on the factual character of the physical or bodily resurrection and virginal conception, "though," he continues immediately, "none of them holds them to be essential." Mascall's remark is justified. It is incredible, in van Buren's mind, to consider them as facts of history. Robinson declares himself to be open-minded on the biological details of the birth narrative; he is indifferent to the historic factuality of the empty tomb. By implication certainly, a similar indifference expresses the attitude of Cox.

For our present purposes, it is Secularization's generalizing simplification itself that merits attention. We might best approach the problem by considering two impressions, both incorrect, that could easily be caught at this point, especially by students. We note the first of these in criticism of the new radical theology; and we note the second in equally frank criticism of Mascall.

Now even though the movement which we are treating is not really a movement of or within biblical theology, it does overlap with certain topics of biblical theology, and the matter of historic factuality is obviously one of them. Also, we have to bear in mind the natural effect of the wide, and often just as inaccurate, reporting that has given Secularization, especially as confused with *Death of God,* so much currency. For this means, among other things, that the peculiar way the new theology frames the perennial question of historicity might be presumed to be the latest, and now taken for granted, way. Finally, there is the attractiveness, quite understandable, of the simplification. People enjoying at least a cursory familiarity with the historicity problem in biblical theology are not infrequently overwhelmed by the complexity of the problem, as likewise by the bulk and nuance of scholarly opinion. But now, it would seem, the picture clarifies.

In such a context, one confronted by Secularization's simple break with everything "other-worldly" might say to himself, "This is the last straw. But it is a relief to get it over with. I guess this is where modern biblical criticism was heading all along." Such a person is thinking, of course, of the progressive chipping away at biblical fact that has been going on now for a long, long time—even, if reluctantly, in all but the most naïvely fundamentalist traditional Christian theology. The seven days of Genesis were a way of making a point. The talking serpent was another. There may not have been any real Magi. An Annunciation "scene" probably never took place. So why, he asks, retard a process whose eventual conclusion is so perfectly clear?

The impression is understandable. Something like this, or at least not altogether unlike this, has been happening. But the impression is also very wide of the mark. It is the natural effect of too much oversimplification.

First, a chipping-away process (though this may not be too good a name for it) has undoubtedly accompanied the biblical scholar's steadily increasing awareness of the existence and implications of literary genre. Thus, to come straight to the point, the Gospel accounts are what many today would like to call "confessional" literature. But even this is inadequate. For the Gospels, as a literary class, are a class to themselves. In any case, and this is here and now the important consideration, the Gospel literature is emphatically not "reportorial." This does not deny van Buren's insistence that the Gospels nevertheless do contain an element of informative communication. It merely means that the controlling thrust of this genre of writing is a special kind of "bearing witness," and this rather than any recognizable kind of biographical or historical reportage.

If and when the critical evidence requires it, therefore, one is in no way prevented from abandoning the rigorously "factual" reading, say, of Matthew's Sermon on the Mount. A pattern of "sermon" introduced by appropriate narrative is clearly the organization principle behind the greater portion of this particular Gospel. Hence, one could consider a first, and not very startling, departure from historic factuality, and interpret the Sermon on the Mount as a literary device whereby many of the sayings of Jesus were collected into a convenient and expressive unity. But the "sayings," to go a further step, would not necessarily have to be even sayings. It is quite possible that the final redactor, relying upon both traditional material and his own originality, has composed much of the detail himself. The "sayings," therefore, could be merely a neat way of summarizing Jesus' teaching, and of conveying in a concrete manner his religious spirit. Nor is there any decisive *a priori* argument, to take up a more delicate matter, against an author's use of *vaticinium ex eventu,* always as legitimate and communicative literary style. Thus Mark, in a key passage, quotes at least indirectly the "words" of Jesus at Caesarea Philippi referring to his death and resurrection after three days. It is possible that on the actual occasion Jesus had spoken at least less precisely and in less detail.

The last mentioned example, however, affords an opportunity for making an important observation. It is true, on the one hand, that the contemporary exegete's greater understanding of what is peculiar to the Gospel genre has encouraged the "defactualizing" process just noted. It is not true, on the other hand, and as the impression might exist, that a total "defactualizing" is just around the corner. A few decades ago, the trend was to argue that Jesus certainly made no reference to the three days, nor to his rising again, nor perhaps even to the Son of man who must suffer many things. The trend today, however, is to allow that he very definitely spoke of the Son of man who must suffer many things, and also, since he identified himself in this way not only with the Son of man but also with the Suffering Servant, he not unlikely spoke, at least in some fashion, of both the death and subsequent exaltation of Deutero-Isaiah's Suffering

Servant as well. In a number of respects, therefore, "defactualiz-ing" has actually encountered a strictly academic and scientific reaction.

Secondly, however, a chipping-away process does have to be recorded in one particular area, that of the miraculous interven-tion and apparition. As we remarked earlier, the new radical theology has only the one category of the "other-worldly." Tra-ditional Christianity, on the other hand, would speak distinctly of the divine, of the supernatural (which is intervention only in a special sense), and of the preternatural or the miraculous. That some such distinction has, in fact, to be made now becomes clear.

For the writers of the Old Testament in general, just about everything that happened in this world aside from sin was due to the direct intervention of Yahweh in the affairs of men. With such a mentality, it was perfectly normal to describe natural and human events in the embellished idiom of the super-earthly marvel. It was the hand of Yahweh that spread the waters and crumbled the city walls, that visited men with pestilence and then with cure.

By comparison, the New Testament is much more down to earth. But something of the super-earthly marvel could be seen as retained: in the moving star, in the voice from the heavens, in the walking upon the waters, in the healings and prophecies of Jesus, and of course in his miraculous birth and resurrection. The trouble with putting all these things together, however, is that they do not belong together. The star and the voice were most likely symbolic devices employed by the Evangelists to communicate, or to help communicate, the mystery of the in-carnation and Servant commission of Jesus. The walkings and the healings and the prophecies, such of these as we are meant to take literally, so to speak, would have been in any case marvels of a unique order: the extraordinary or preternatural doings of one who was at the same time God, and performed exclusively in the context, the strictly supernatural and not merely preternatural context, of his incarnation and redemption. Much more decisively still, is this the context for the birth and the resurrection.

Yet, we said that there was evidence of something like a chipping away at least in the area of the preternatural marvel. Yes. In our judgment, even present-day traditional Christianity tends to make progressively less and less of the marvel—that is, of the marvel which is not unequivocally immediate to the redeeming life of Christ and the sanctifying indwelling of the Spirit in the Church and its members. Another way of saying this would be to suggest that the marvel is coming more and more to be recognized as not God's way of dealing with men. Today, then, things like the star and the voice are far less apt to be assigned factual reality in the ordinary sense. Nor is the tendency restricted to biblical exegesis. Today, miracles and private revelations are not denied. No. But they are being made very much less of. One need only contrast, for example, the attitude of present-day Roman Catholics toward Fatima with that of their grandfathers toward Lourdes.

On the other side, there is no evidence at all of a chipping away in either the supernatural (stricter sense) or the divine. To say this with such confidence may cause surprise, even to Roman Catholics. What we are witnessing in modern Catholic theology, however, is not a diminishing of the supernatural, nor even a suppression of the distinction between the supernatural and the natural. What we are witnessing is rather a tendency to correct both the notion and the distinction, and to do so in terms of the insights of contemporary biblical criticism. The "supernatural" in this process is becoming more and more synonymous with the "specifically Christian," and the "natural" more and more synonymous with the "specifically human." In his Christ, and through identification with his Christ, God is still calling men to share in his own divine life. Further, as the supernatural becomes more and more dissociated from the preternatural and the marvel, it is becoming less and less "other-worldly." Thus, there is not, today, so much of an inclination to separate the natural and the supernatural, or to envision man as somehow living in two worlds at once. He lives here. And he lives here with the option, not the automatic necessity, of identification with Christ. If he accepts it, then the "specifically human" in him is no longer solely that, but becomes fused with the "specifically Christian," and he thinks of being "truly human" and "specifically Christian" as interchangeable. But not if he rejects it. Such an interplay of the human and the Christian, moreover, is recognized not only among Catholics, but throughout Christianity. That is why we can say that there has not been, in fact, any progressive chipping away in the supernatural. The chipping, we have to observe, belongs today, no less than in the past, to Christianity's fringe.

And so too, in the final inspection, does any chipping away in the divine. The Godhood of Christ—in some equivalent formula, and beginning with the ancient confession "Jesus is Lord"—has ever been proclaimed by all but minority groups within the Christian community. Even when and where there has been hesitation, this has been far more often at the appropriateness of a formulary than at what is essential to the confession. Oddly, a great exception to this, if there really is one at all, would not be that of the present moment, when someone might want to point to all the "statistical" Christians who do not accept the Godhood of Christ, but that of the fourth century, which prompted Jerome to exclaim that "the whole world groaned to find itself Arian." For the Arians were Christians in serious intention, and also, at least at the surface and the level of the formulary, deniers of divinity. One could question, however, the actuality of the denial in the countless hordes of political Arians included in Jerome's "whole world." But one could even more easily question the actuality of a serious intention to be Christian in the many today who do not seem to give a thought to it except when asked to indicate sectarian affiliation.

There is, then, no foundation for the fear that the same progressive and widely accepted cutting away process which first took the Magi now endangers the resurrection. There is, of course, a present-day problem with regard to the resurrection, and it is not at all confined to the radical fringe. This is the problem of the resurrection as physical or corporal in relation to historic fact, and we shall discuss this problem in a moment. But the resurrection, we must repeat, was the resurrection of one who was divine, and it was the key mystery, or mystery-event, of the strictly supernatural, the specifically Christian, new creation. It does not therefore belong with the preternatural or the marvel. Hence, if contemporary Christianity tends to make much less of the marvel, this really has no automatic bearing on the resurrection.

The impression of a "no end to it" that might be created by the new radical theology's simple dismissal of everything "otherworldly," therefore, cannot be allowed to stand. But neither can another erroneous impression, likewise encouraged by the new radical theology, and, in the writer's judgment, unintentionally aggravated rather than displaced by Mascall's reply. This is the impression that Christian theology, in all but its most radical forms, continues to speak glibly and naïvely about "historical fact."

To be sure, different theologians and different schools speak about historical fact in different ways. There is nothing like a universally, or even widely, accepted network of qualifications and distinctions. One fairly common notion, however, is that of the "meta-historical," and it is neither a meaningless gimmick nor a piece of theological sophism. It is applicable, and quite significantly so, to the problem of the bodily resurrection.

In the strict sense of history, that is, in the sense of the science which goes by that name, a risen body cannot be part of "historical fact." This does not mean at all that a risen body cannot be real; it simply means that it cannot be real with the type or class of reality properly called historical fact. For the only human body that history, the science, knows, and can possibly deal with as historical fact, is the only body that this world, in the entire course of its evolution, has ever been able to support: and that body is the body that dies. The body, on the other hand, that does not die, that is henceforth immortal, is outside the time-space continuum of history's world. In this very precise sense, therefore, it cannot be classified with historical fact. The closest history can come to such a body is to the human testimony, if such there be, that witnesses to its reality. But the body itself is not an object that can be handled by historical tools.

But is not this just another way of saying that a risen body is, therefore, an "other-worldly" body in the new theology's sense of "other-worldly"? In the final analysis, not at all. The risen body is, by definition so to speak, material. To say this, however, and to say it without qualification, can be misleading. For the risen body, precisely as free from the laws of our material universe, does not belong to the order of our material universe. Rather, it belongs to the order of the divine as operating the economy of salvation, to the order, therefore, that is centered in Christ, made present to human history in the humanity of Jesus of Nazareth, but at the same time transcending that humanity. Historical empiricism, moreover, can say nothing about such an order: neither to establish, nor to disprove, it. Such an order, however, the order of the *total* Christ, is far from what the new theology has in mind when it uses the term "other-worldly." "Other-worldly" is equivalent, actually, to "*deus ex machina.*" It is God and divine intervention conceived precisely as filling the gaps in human knowledge that science had long left open but has now succeeded in closing. The "other-worldly" is simply that which takes the place of the empirical where the substitution is no longer required and has become a scientific and intellectual nuisance. The "other-worldly," when all is said and done, is what is declared emphatically to be not of this world, but what is nevertheless assigned a strictly worldly function and made accessible to strictly worldly observation. The empiricist can hardly be blamed for having little patience with the "other-worldly" as thus conceived. He can well be blamed, however, for presuming that this is always and automatically the conception.

Yet, it is extremely important to give the empiricist his full score. Mascall, for all the intended fairness and care of his debate with van Buren, does not really do this. His own idiom and pattern of analysis remains throughout that of history and fact and the fact of history—without nuance. But this only helps to strengthen the impression that Christian theology's sole alternative to the radical empiricism is precisely the theological historicism that the empiricist presumed it to be. And this is unfortunate.

In the chapter in *The Secularization of Christianity* that bears the title of the book itself, Mascall is quite severe in his criticism of what van Buren makes of Easter. Easter becomes, and becomes exclusively, what happened to the disciples, not what happened to Jesus. And Mascall cites the reason: "It would, we must note, be foreign to van Buren's whole position to enquire whether the Easter faith itself may have been due to the actual occurrence of certain supernatural events within human history; by definition no such events could be part of 'history'." "History" here is strictly empirical history. The function of Mascall's inverted commas is to draw attention to history as van Buren understands it. But history as van Buren understands it, and calls empirical history, is the history which we ourselves have been referring to as that of the science which goes by the name.

Two observations, then, seem to be in order. First, Mascall is quite correct in arguing against van Buren that Easter cannot possibly be reduced to nothing more than what happened to the disciples, that is to say, to their new experience of Jesus in the contagion of his freedom. For Easter is first and foremost the resurrection of Jesus himself. The message of Easter is that he really is raised from the dead, in his glorified body and in the full splendor of his divinity. The only qualification that might be appended, if someone wants to say that Easter is first what "happened" to Jesus, is that "happened" here is being used in an extended sense. Normally, the context of the word is strictly empirical, but this time it is not. Secondly, however, it is van Buren who is correct in claiming that such content of the Gospel Easter message simply cannot be considered as historical fact in the ordinary sense of history. Mascall, on the other hand, apparently sees no difficulty in speaking of "the actual occurrence of certain supernatural events within human history."

Now Mascall is by no means a fundamentalist. In his final chapter, he explicitly repudiates the fundamentalist notion of the Gospels as "a bare 'photographic' and 'tape-recorded' account of the acts and words of our Lord." But this is not enough. It does not meet van Buren's challenge. The problem is not merely that the Gospels contain interpretative statements as well as factual statements, which van Buren in any case admits, but that among the seemingly factual statements there are some that cannot be factual statements, in the usual sense, at all. Mascall contests this last. But to our mind he need not, and should not, do so. Van Buren's language is precise. In the present context, he is taking factual and historical as empirically factual and empirically historical. And a risen body is not empirically factual or empirically historical. If one wants to speak of the resurrection, therefore, as either "factual" or "historical," the expression has to be somehow nuanced.

As we remarked earlier, however, what Secularization might say about the resurrection is not really what is distinctive of the movement. What is distinctive of the movement in its tearing down or reductionist phase is its dismissal of the "other-worldly" —as a unit, we might say, and totally, whether by simple denial or by deliberate and systematic preterition. And in this dismissal of everything "other-worldly," the more serious and more characteristic problem of Secularization is not historic factuality so much as objective reality, especially the objective reality of God.

B. God and Objective Reality

We have already seen that both Robinson and Cox acknowledge the reality of God, and even the true divinity of Christ. With neither, therefore, is there any question of denying God. But there is some question of ignoring him. Robinson wants to make use of Tillich, so that the transcendent God of Christianity will at least cease to be "up there," "out there," or in short, "other-worldly." Perhaps more indicative of the bishop's ultimate cast of mind, however, is his rephrasing of Bonhoeffer on the question "Must Christianity be 'Religious'?" It is in Robinson's second chapter entitled with a question mark "The End of Theism?" "Bonhoeffer's answer is that we should boldly discard 'the religious premise', as St. Paul had the courage to jettison circumcision as a precondition of the Gospel, and accept 'the world's coming of age' as a God-given fact. 'The only way to be honest is to recognize that we have to live in the world *etsi deus non daretur*'—even if God is not 'there'. Like children outgrowing the secure religious, moral and intellectual framework of the home, in which 'Daddy' is always there in the background, 'God is teaching us that we must live as men who can get along very well without him'." And Cox, in the very second paragraph of his introduction, writes: "Secularization is man turning his attention away from worlds beyond and toward this world and this time (*saeculum* = 'this present age'). It is what Dietrich Bonhoeffer in 1944 called 'man's coming of age'."

This is what we have called the deliberate and systematic preterition. God is not denied, briefly affirmed in fact, but then set aside. For Robinson, the preoccupying interest is henceforth with the New Testament Jesus as the here and now utterly human "man for others." Cox's concern is rather to show that the world itself, this world, and precisely in its secularization, *is* God: not in any pantheistic sense, of course, but in the sense that the secularized world itself, in its shape, its style, its energies, its virtues, is God's authentic self-manifestation for our time; but even this is said without any intended prejudice to the Judaeo-Christian revelation of God, or to his Christ, insofar as the last norm of the "secular city's" spiritual creativeness is its identification with both.

There is a negative or reductionist element, then, in Robinson, and it is often vociferous. Similarly, though much more quietly, there is a negative or reductionist element in Cox. Nevertheless, the prevailing attitude in each case, and especially that of Cox, is positive and constructive. Cox, moreover, as we have already seen, offers a painstaking and articulate definition of secularization. In the chapter immediately following, therefore, we propose to return to that definition in order to examine in greater detail its basic evolutionist insight. And that is the context in which we shall want to discuss Cox's reductionism, the reductionism of a systematic preterition governed by a principle of total immanentism.

At the moment, however, our attention has to be given to the more straightforward and radical reductionism of *The Secular Meaning of the Gospel.* Van Buren does not acknowledge, and then pass over, the transcendent God of objective reality. He refuses to talk about him at all—and goes to great length to explain why. Ultimately, the reason he refuses is because it is meaningless to do so. Modern "empirically minded" man can see nothing but a waste of time in trying to talk about something which the laws of human language have irreversibly struck from the agenda. The challenge here is a serious one, all the more so since, as even Mascall concedes, van Buren argues his case with a very high degree of scholarly competence.

In our own introductory chapter, we traced the movement of

van Buren's presentation through the extremely important first 50 pages of Part Two. Our immediate purpose was to come to grips at an early stage with the question whether or not van Buren's position was atheist. We must now return to those same passages, and use them as the proper jumping off spot for getting to the bottom of the author's reductionist argument.

Paul van Buren is a very neat writer. His title, taken in the context of present-day theology's even more popular dialogue, puts his reader in possession of the broad scope of the undertaking. *The Secular Meaning of the Gospel* is going to be a reinterpretation or reconstruction along explicitly declared "secular" lines of the Gospel message. Parts One and Two divide clearly and conventionally. Part One gives the reason for the undertaking, plus the method to be employed: this is what others have been saying on the point; this is what the author finds wanting on the one hand, suggestive on the other; against such a background he sets up his own ground rules. Part Two accomplishes the undertaking, works out the actual reinterpretation or reconstruction. And the first 50 pages of Part Two would seem to contain the heart of the matter. For the reconstruction begins, as we would expect, with the historic personality of Jesus of Nazareth, with the Easter phenomenon, with the impact of Easter upon the primitive Christian community and the condensed expression of this impact in the community's most ancient and basic confession "Jesus is Lord." As a matter of fact, this opening section of Part Two does contain the heart of van Buren's reconstruction, but only inasmuch as its statements and conclusions are understood in the full light of the methodological principles laid down in Part One, especially in its fourth and final chapter.

Yet, there is apt to be a difficulty here. As a teacher of some modest experience, we would not be surprised if more than an occasional reader of van Buren's study skipped rather lightly over precisely the methodological section just mentioned. The very name "linguistic analysis" is all that some would need to see to quicken their pace into the biblical part coming up. If they follow such an impulse, however, they run the risk of recognizing in Part Two little more than still another Gospel reinterpretation of the, roughly speaking, Bultmannian type: that is to say, a reduction of the supranatural or "other worldly," plus a sophisticated and naturalistic restatement.

But this would be to miss van Buren's point in two decisive ways. First, van Buren's Gospel reconstruction is a *Christ*ology, not a *theo*logy. We had already observed van Buren's criticism of Bultmann for having failed to ground Christianity, or at least to do so adequately, upon the historical Jesus of Nazareth. Secondly, van Buren's reconstruction not only makes more of Christ than of God, but actually excludes God. The question of the moment, then, is in the why: or better, in the why behind the why behind the why that takes us back into the discussion about method.

Apart from the exclusion of God and the reasoning processes supporting it, there is little if anything really distinctive in van Buren's reconstruction. In a sense, moreover, even the traditionalist could accept it, or much of it, at least in principle. If he did not have to exclude God from the exegesis, nor the divinity of Christ, there would be no *a priori* motive against interpreting Easter in respect to its impact upon the disciples as their experience of Jesus' freedom. Van Buren, however, is not merely saying that it is that; he is saying that it is that and only that. His brief summary in the middle of the sixth chapter makes his position absolutely clear: "The foregoing interpretation of the history of Jesus, Easter, and of the Gospel provides a logical account of the language of Christian faith without resort to a misleading use of words. The word 'God' has been avoided because it equivocates and misleads. It seems to be a proper name, calling up the image of a divine entity, but it refuses to function as any other proper name does. Circumlocutions such as 'transcendence', 'being', and 'absolute' only evade but do not overcome the difficulty."

In van Buren's own words, therefore, what is noteworthy about his reconstruction of the Gospel is that it avoids all mention of the word "God," as also of what he considers to be the deceptively evasive substitutions. This is no less than what he had told us that he was going to do back in the passage entitled "A Method for Reconstruction" which concluded Part One: "In the frank recognition that the lot of oblique language about God is not better, and in some ways worse, than that of simple literal theism, we come face to face with our real problem of understanding the Gospel today: the difficulty of finding any meaningful way to speak of God. We can no longer share the faith of the man who thought that his god lived in a tree and that his god would die if the tree were burned down. . . . We should say that he was mistaken, but his religious assertions were understandable. An assertion of qualified literal theism, on the other hand, is meaningless. . . . Miles's suggestion of silence is very much in order at this point, and if theology at its best has not meant to infringe on this silence, its reticence has not always been obvious." Van Buren himself, however, will keep silent. He will not allow himself to use the *word,* the word "God." For, as he adds at the end of the second paragraph further on, "today, we cannot even understand the Nietzschean cry that 'God is dead!' for if it were so, how could we know? No, the problem now is that the *word* 'God' is dead."

Thus it is quite clear—the first why in the series—why van Buren must attempt to reinterpret the Gospel without mentioning God, without even uttering the word. It is because the word is meaningless. But why is it meaningless? If we wanted to answer this second why in the same direct fashion as the first, we could say that for van Buren the word "God" and statements about "God" are meaningless because they cannot be verified empirically. But this might be to get a little ahead of ourselves.

Van Buren grounds his assertion of the meaninglessness of "God," first upon a broad appeal to the present-day empirical mentality, and only then and in this more general context upon use of empirical verification as understood by the linguistic analysts in particular.

The author's candor here is impressive. He does not come up to us and say that as a result of certain highly specialized and recondite experiments which he has been conducting in the language laboratory he can now prove to us the ultimate meaninglessness of talking about God. What he says, rather, is simply that he is an "empirically minded" man, adding, but without any pomposity, that a thoughtful and honest person—today—really has no other choice than to be "empirically minded." Such a person can no longer tolerate the talk about God because he can no longer tolerate *any* kind of talk that takes place, so to put it, outside the evidence, outside the way of speaking that is normal in everything else, outside the scientific and secular world as we now know it. This is the real crux of van Buren's argument. He keeps reminding us of the fact as he refers constantly, but loosely, to the "empirical attitudes" which he has come to make his own.

Nevertheless, what we might venture to call the argument from attitude can still be given logical form and precision. For in the world today, there is at least one group of individuals who not only share these empirical attitudes, but have brought them to bear precisely upon the language of faith and religion and the talk about God. This is the relatively small group of linguistic analysts, British in the main, who have been practicing for some time now on theology's fringe. In van Buren's eyes, what is most significant in the contribution of this group is that, of all those who continue today to discuss the problem of God, they and they alone confront the problem at its roots. "God" is a word, a piece of human language, and the empirical linguistic analysts have exposed the meaninglessness of that word. In so doing, they have set the stage for the necessarily Godless reconstruction of the Christian Gospel.

Van Buren moves in two steps. First, he wants to show us what is ultimately insufficient in every other theology except the linguistic empiricism of his own sympathies. This is quite a task, and it will be uphill all the way. For van Buren's charge of having missed the real point is directed not only against the traditionalists, but also against the strictly modern schools which tend to be considered "far out" and which enjoy wide popularity in radical circles. Secondly, he wants to introduce us to the corrective insights of the linguistic analysts.

If van Buren feels that all but the linguistic analysts are missing the point, it must be something particular. And, of course, it is. The point, again, is the talk about God, the very possibility of such talk. More accurately, it is the talk about God and the possibility of such talk as introduced into the talk about Jesus. Van Buren's study, we have to remember, is a Christology. His immediate purpose is not to discuss the problem of God, nor to debunk God, but to reconstruct, in whatever way proves necessary, the Gospel of Jesus.

Now for the traditionally minded, there is not going to be this sort of Jesus and God issue here. Talk about Jesus is automatically talk about God, because Jesus *is* God. Van Buren, however, would prefer to say that Jesus *became* God, and precisely because the talk about Jesus was turned into the talk about God—but need never have been.

In this fashion, van Buren gets into his historical second chapter, the first chapter in Part One. It all happened, he begins to explain, between the second and fifth centuries, between Justin Martyr and Chalcedon. The Alexandrian Fathers concentrating on John 1:14 ("And the Word became flesh and dwelt among us") gradually came to identify Jesus of Nazareth as the incarnation of the divine Logos. The decision at Nicaea in 325 was final: the Logos, the Eternal Word, was "consubstantial" with the Father, and therefore divine unequivocally. So the talk about Jesus became talk about God.

But did it not remain at the same time talk about man? Was not Jesus' true humanity affirmed just as emphatically—at Chalcedon—as his true divinity? Yes. In van Buren's mind, however, the yes here must not be glib. It is true, on the one hand, that the Antiochene Fathers, in reaction against extreme forms of Alexandrianism, and especially that of Apollinarism, continued to stress Jesus' true humanity along with his possession of a truly human psychology. And it was the twofold element, as also the uncompromised unity of the God-Man, that was eventually given expression in the famous Decree of Chalcedon in 451: Jesus, the Eternal Word, is both perfectly God and perfectly man, one undivided person in two natures, the divine and the human. On the other hand, as van Buren sees it, it is likewise true that the perfect humanity so clearly affirmed by Chalcedon never ceased to be, at least in practice, something less than that, or something more. In the last analysis, the humanity of patristic Christology was always a qualified and privileged humanity overshadowed by divinity. In this sense, the talk about Jesus, even when it was about Jesus in his humanity, was still lost in the talk about God.

Yet, for van Buren, all this need never have happened. He does not blame the Fathers, much less excoriate them. Van Buren, in fact, and notwithstanding his dislike of metaphysics, is quite free from the sort of historically uncritical, if not amateurish, blast against the hellenization of the Christian Gospel which we encounter so often in modern theology. The Fathers, as he judges them, were at least true to their own insights, and we might follow their example in being equally true to ours. It was inevitable, given their times and intellectual background, that the Fathers would interpret the Word being made flesh and the Word dwelling among us ontologically. Thus Logos Christology became divinity and divine nature Christology. Talk about

Jesus became talk about God. In principle, however, it need not have happened. The Gospel itself had suggested another alternative.

Van Buren's consideration of this alternative sets in motion the first of the two main steps indicated a short while back. He has presented the problem, and he has presented it in historical context. *De facto,* talk about Jesus has become talk about God. Originally this was due to the Gospel interpretation of the Fathers. With such an introduction and state of the question, van Buren can now turn to the contemporary theological dialogue. As he does so, his attention is focussed primarily upon two groups: first, Bultmann and the existentialists; secondly, the linguistic analysts.

There is, however, a short but important interval before van Buren takes up the existentialists. His purpose is to include, at least briefly, the whole of the contemporary Christian theology. He achieves this through a sort of *a fortiori.* He by no means plans to examine what every Christian sect, and every Christian school, has to say about the Gospel Jesus. Rather, van Buren comes, as he sees it, straight to the point. Present-day biblical theology in general, and quite aside from Bultmann and the existentialists, has already confronted the problem caused by the patristic exegesis. It has shown, as we shall discuss immediately, that the ontological interpretation was neither the only alternative nor the one closest to a scientifically critical reading of the Gospel text.

Of course, van Buren will then go on, this by itself is not enough. At the general level, contemporary biblical theology has gone only so far. And we might mention at this point van Buren's rather incisive dismissal of biblical theology in an article published much more recently, April 7, 1965, in *The Christian Century.* Ultimately, modern man wants a Gospel that *he* can understand, a Gospel whose significant message is restated in terms that are meaningful to a scientific and intellectually sophis-

ticated society, and made relevant to its secular condition. Bultmann and the existentialists go further, therefore, though, as
van Buren will continue to press the issue, still not far enough,
nor always in the right direction.

We note, then, the *a fortiori* operating here: if present-day
Christian theology at the height of its scientific respectability
(= biblical theology in general) and at the presumable extreme
of its radical "this-worldliness" (= Bultmann and the existentialists) offers no adequate solution to the problem of the Gospel Jesus, much less does it do so at any level more traditionalist
or more conservative. Thus van Buren can restrict his account
of the contemporary dialogue to modern biblical theology in
general and to Bultmann and the existentialists in particular.
The *a fortiori*, however, carries at least one serious qualification.
As we have observed heretofore, van Buren's attitude toward
one aspect, but a vital aspect, of the Bultmannian achievement
is that it was really no achievement at all. He considers Bultmann's down-playing of historicity neither a scientific nor secularist advance over traditionalism, but rather a move that was as
ill-grounded critically as it might have been radical in its ambi-
tion. But this exception once made, the present-day Christian
theology which van Buren finds pertinent reduces to biblical
theology in general and Bultmannianism in particular.

The contribution of biblical theology, then, is introduced in
the context of the patristic exegesis. For the Fathers, talk about
Jesus had to be talk about God—in a sense and to a degree,
even when they were talking about the human nature. Modern
biblical theology sees it otherwise.

In the New Testament, Jesus is called, it is true, the Son of
God, who came from God, and is one with the Father. The modern Christian, under the influence of the tradition that goes
back to the Fathers, is usually inclined to think of these biblical
references as designating natural sonship, eternal origin understood substantially, and unity in essence. But if he were aware

of what is now recognized by today's even more conservative biblical theology, and van Buren makes a rather telling use of Oscar Cullmann at this point, he would see that the original language had been spoken in quite a different context. The title "Son of God" in the Old Testament designated Israel itself, and then individuals, such as the king and the high priest, who represented the Covenant people in a special way. The title, in its first and immediate signification, indicated "serving obedience," and it is precisely in the same context, Covenant context, of serving obedience that it becomes in the New Testament a title of Jesus. Jesus is Son of God inasmuch as he has been called by God to execute a unique commission in the Covenant relationship, and has responded to this call with unique fidelity.

The same idea lies at the base of the Gospel references to his "coming from God." For as we see in John 9:29–33, Moses, too, can be thought of as "coming from God." This is because Moses is a man to whom God "has spoken." Thus, it is not necessary to interpret Jesus' coming from God along the patristic lines of the eternal and substantial origin of the divine Logos. "To be 'from God'," van Buren sums up, "is to be a man to whom God has spoken and who is obedient to Yahweh's will." The context established by the Old Testament background is once again that of call and response. Finally, John 10:30–38 shows that this same context is the key to the meaning of such apparently ontological references to Jesus as his being "one with" the Father, "in" the Father, and as having the Father "in" himself. Each of these expressions is equivalent in meaning to the title "Son of God," which is the same as being one who does the "work" of God as one to whom the "word" of God has been spoken.

There is, then, van Buren concludes, an alternative to the patristic interpretation. Not even the Johannine Prologue stands in opposition to this alternative. "Yahweh's decision expresses his very heart. The prologue to the Gospel of John summarizes this idea by saying that God's word is God himself, from the 'beginning'. It was possible to identify Yahweh with his decision because the New Testament authors conceived of God always in relation to the decision enacted in Jesus of Nazareth. In the beginning there was the decision that there should be one for the many, and that the many should come to know themselves to be involved with the one. And 'in the fullness of time', this purpose was enacted concretely in the history of Jesus of Nazareth. It became flesh, a plan enacted, and Yahweh's purpose dwelt among us in that Jesus dwelt among men. What Yahweh had to say to man, what he had in mind for men, was to be heard and seen in the form of this man, who was, therefore, the very word of Yahweh."

The reader will note that van Buren is not right now saying anything about the problem of God. Nor is he even saying anything about the elements of biblical mythology, as the existentialists speak of it, that the foregoing interpretation based upon the concepts of "call" and "response" leaves intact. Yahweh remains, and he continues to intervene in the affairs of men. For now, van Buren merely wants to draw attention to the fact that contemporary biblical theology in general has already broken away from the "divinity" exegesis of the Fathers. Jesus, even as Logos, can be interpreted differently. This is, to be sure, only a beginning, but nevertheless an important beginning.

By way of comment before going on with the rest of van Buren's argument, we would offer the following. First, van Buren is quite correct to the extent that he makes his point for "another alternative" positively but not also exclusively. There could be some dispute, of course, on certain matters of detail: on whether, for example, we can assign so wide a role to Covenant theology in the New, as distinct from the Old, Testament; or whether we can accept van Buren's "plan enacted" as doing sufficient justice to the peculiar overtones of "flesh" (*sarx*) in John 1:14. But such matters of detail are not the real issue

here. In the main and in principle, the author's alternative reflects accurately the insistence of present-day biblical theology
upon the literal sense as determined by the actual consciousness
of the sacred writer. Thus, the exegesis is basically valid. As a
matter of fact, it *is* exegesis, whereas the patristic exegesis was
not exegesis, in the modern usage, to begin with; rather, it was
theological interpretation, or as Bernard Lonergan prefers to
say, more precisely it was theological understanding.

Secondly, however, while van Buren does not at this stage in
his argument simply rule out the patristic interpretation, nevertheless he does deprive it of any necessity. And this raises a
problem, even a problem of having faithfully reported on the
conclusions of present-day biblical theology. For the biblical
theologian is quite willing to accept "serving obedience" as the
immediate literal point of the "Son of God" texts. He is also
willing to admit that the New Testament does not simply
"teach" divinity; this is neither the idiom nor the pattern of
thought. But the biblical theologian, whether liberal or conservative, is going to add that nevertheless the New Testament
writers took Jesus to be God—did so consciously, moreover. If
and when and as the question regarding divinity is raised, therefore, yes is the only answer we can conclude from the ensemble
of what the New Testament writers actually thought and wrote.
That such a mind was implicit in their confession "Jesus is
Lord" is admitted even by the radical biblical theologian who
will want to subsume immediately: "but in this they were
wrong." Van Buren is not correct, therefore, in citing contemporary biblical theology's alternative precisely as a substitute pure
and simple. Yet, this would seem to be his intention.

Thirdly and finally, however, the ultimate problem here is,
of course, van Buren's conviction, derived from non-exegetical
and non-biblical sources, that to talk about God is meaningless.
At the moment, he is not discussing this conviction directly, but
it does motivate the suggestion of exclusivism in his "call–

response" interpretation. To engage him precisely on this further point, we shall first have to let him complete his argument.

There is, then, an initial break. The talk about Jesus did not have to become talk about God. The Logos could and should have been seen as the one specially elected by God to fulfill a unique commission in the Covenant partnership. For modern man, however, this is still too much. If the Gospel must nevertheless retain the mythological world-picture in which it was presented, retain its miracles and its supranatural interventions, modern man will push it aside. But it is exactly to prevent him from doing so, that the existentialist "Left" invites him to distinguish between the myth and the message.

This still further and explicitly liberal attempt to meet the contemporary need is the subject of van Buren's third chapter. It is here that he discusses the contribution of Rudolf Bultmann. More accurately, it is here that he treats of Bultmann as restated and "corrected" by Schubert Ogden.

The Secular Meaning of the Gospel does not offer anything even remotely approaching a detailed account, much less analysis, of the Bultmannian theology. This poses a bit of a problem, inasmuch as one is normally expected these days to work with the text, all the more so when criticism of an individual or a movement is going to be largely unfavorable. In van Buren's defense, however, two things might be observed. First, the text in this instance is really Ogden's *Christ Without Myth,* and van Buren follows it carefully. As van Buren had indicated in his introductory first chapter, Ogden's study focusses upon both Bultmann himself and the debate to which he gave rise at the point where what is most seriously in question is Bultmann's basic methodological consistency. This is just the matter which van Buren wishes to take up: not the detail of Bultmann's New Testament reinterpretation, but the methodological restrictions which had already predetermined its limits and form. Secondly, van Buren seems to consider the main insights governing Bultmann's original proposal as something which contemporary theology has now assimilated and can henceforth take for granted. The generalization would include himself, and despite the severity of his criticisms. The need of the present day, van Buren heartily agrees, *is* to make the Gospel message relevant to modern scientific and secular man, —at least in some sense, therefore, to reduce, transpose, reinterpret. Van Buren even grants that Bultmann's program was not entirely lacking either in empiricist orientation or in concern for language.

Yet, van Buren certainly believes that the Bultmann–Ogden reinterpretation, while we can learn much from many of its suggestions, nevertheless has no future. When all is said and done, it retains too much of the "other-worldly" on the one hand, too little of the Gospel on the other.

For the existentialist Left, the message of the Christian Gospel reduces, on demythologizing analysis, wholly and simply to the proclamation of man's original possibility for authentic existence. Its statements are not intended to inform, or to present some sort of picture of the universe. In this sense, they are neither historical nor cosmological. Positively, the statements of the Gospel narrative through which the proclamation is conveyed are actually intended to incite to action: in a highly imaginative, concrete fashion, the hearer is being encouraged, impelled, to take possession of himself at the root and meaning of his existence, and to live accordingly.

But an immediate problem arises. What is thus exposed as the demythologized essence of the Gospel proclamation, this original possibility of authentic existence, would certainly seem to antedate the Gospel, and to be, in fact, independent of the Gospel. On the other hand, van Buren in his Introduction had already noted Bultmann's "concern to put the kerygma, stripped of its mythological form and interpreted existentially, at the center of faith and theology. Faith is dependent upon the event of Jesus Christ, his appearance in history, his words and death. Although, according to Bultmann, an existentialist analysis of man can discover something of man's problem, and even define what an authentic existence would be, the kerygma alone offers man the possibility of this new existence, and the kerygma is grounded in the event of Christ."

The Jesus event, therefore, seems to be at one and the same time both incidental and necessary to Bultmann's religious program. This inconsistency, moreover, has been observed from many sides, both liberal and conservative. Ogden, for his part, tries to correct it in the more radical direction. As van Buren continues, "because the Gospel addresses man as one who is without excuse (Rom 2:1), he [Ogden] argues that man is responsible for his existence before, and apart from, being addressed by the Gospel. This responsibility is grounded in the fact that men are everywhere confronted by manifestations of God's love. If the Gospel were the only effective manifestation of that love, then it would have to say that from the time a man first hears it he is without excuse. Only a genuine possibility makes a man genuinely responsible. The Gospel, however, takes seriously the radical responsibility of man, which it could do only if authentic existence (or faith) were a universal human possibility. Authentic existence, therefore, cannot depend only on the event of Jesus of Nazareth." In van Buren's mind, however, this correction is of dubious value. For Ogden, the Jesus event, while not strictly necessary, is nevertheless " 'the decisive manifestation' of 'the unconditioned gift of God's love', which is the 'ever-present ground and end of all created things'. Why the event of Jesus of Nazareth is 'decisive' is not explained. If Bultmann is mistaken in saying that this event is 'necessary' for faith, is Ogden not equally mistaken in calling it 'decisive'?"

Toward the end of his third chapter, and just before passing on to the linguistic analysts for indications of a more satisfactory approach, van Buren organizes his evaluation of the existentialist Left around five specific points of criticism. The relationship between Secularization and Christian Existentialism is important enough to justify their inclusion in the present study.

By way of preliminary, we should recall to mind the fundamentally different orientation of the two theologies. Bultmann and Ogden are concerned with restoring to modern man a vitalized spirituality centered upon faith in God, or the transcendent. As it happens, so to speak, this God is the God of the Judaeo-Christian revelation. But in their effort to demythologize the Christian Gospel on the one hand, and preserve the transcendent God on the other, the role of the historical Jesus becomes minimized. At least this is the criticism. Van Buren himself, however, does not share the same primary intention. He is not trying to bring the secularist back to God at all. Rather, he is trying to explain to the secularist who is already a Christian, or to the Christian who wakes up to discover that he is a secularist, how one can and should continue to be a Christian, but a Christian who no longer has to think and talk about God. From this perspective, van Buren is naturally going to attack the existentialist Left for retaining too much of the "otherworldly" and too little of the Gospel.

Today, he argues, no religion whatsoever, including Christianity, can possibly have any meaning and value for modern empirically minded man unless it abandons the *entire* "special language" of religious discourse. Such language makes a claim to privilege that is both gratuitous and abhorrent to the scientific and secular mentality. We cannot, therefore, go on, as Bultmann and Ogden have attempted, simply reducing miracle and revelation and supranatural intervention, but nevertheless retaining the idiom and concepts of such things as "experienced non-objective reality," God, the transcendent. In this sense, "religion" is not worth saving. But Christianity is. It is and should be a powerful creative force in contemporary society. In an effort to save "religion," the existentialist Left is prepared to sacrifice Christianity. But this is where the existentialist Left makes the wrong decision. Its attempts, therefore, to reduce the dependence of the Christian religion upon the historical event of Jesus of Nazareth must be resisted just as strongly as its reluctance to have done with the meaningless world of transcendence.

The first of van Buren's five points, then, concerns Ogden's use of the expression "experienced non-objective reality." Bultmann had spoken similarly, but van Buren concedes that he is somewhat uncertain as to whether Ogden's notion is the same as Bultmann's, and as to whether the use of the formula by either author is not perhaps rather flexible. Nonetheless, in the final analysis "they seem to mean 'God', or the 'Transcendent', or (to use Ogden's phrase) 'the unconditioned gift and demand of God's love, which is the ever-present ground and end of all created things'."

Van Buren's criticism of this type of language is quite sharp, and it provides an excellent glimpse of his own basic presuppositions for theological discourse. We use the word "experience" ordinarily in the context of things that can in some way be sensed. But Ogden, following Bultmann, is using it precisely in the context of what cannot be sensed. And this is an illegitimate use of language. The meaning of the formula cannot possibly be verified empirically.

Further, to take van Buren's second and closely connected point, "it is meaningless to speak analogically about God. Bultmann asserts that we may speak of 'God's act' if we do so analogically, on the model of human action and encounter, although actually 'an act of God is not visible to the objectifying eye and cannot be established as can world events'. He rejects a manner of speaking in which the symbol 'God' refers to our own subjective experiences, but he allows that modern man could see God's act 'in an occurrence that grasped him in the reality of his own true life and transformed his own self'. More sharply: 'Man can very well know who God is in the question concerning himself'. In short, Bultmann thinks that 'modern man' can still do something with the word 'God', that there is a way to speak of God both analogically and existentially which man today can understand. Ogden agrees with this."

Van Buren, needless to say, does not. Nor does he see any help in Ogden's observation that statements about God are really statements about man, as in the example "God loves me" = "I feel secure." For as Ogden intends it, this does not mean that the statement about God ceases to be a statement about God and becomes exclusively a statement about man, but rather that the statement about God is simultaneously a statement about *both* God *and* man. This, however, simply brings us back to where we were. The statement as a statement about man is manageable. It is subject to empirical verification. But the same statement as a statement about God is not manageable. Modern man does not know what to do with it. As van Buren concludes, "one wonders where the left wing existentialist theologians have found their 'modern man'. A man who shares the empirical spirit of our age cannot interchange these statements about God and man at all."

The weakness of the existentialist Left, therefore, is a weakness of language, or of linguistic philosophy. This weakness is responsible for the existentialist theology's retention of far too much of the "other-worldly." But the very same weakness, paradoxically, is also responsible for the existentialist theology's reduction of everything that seems to be empirical assertion in the New Testament kerygma to existential proclamation pure and simple. Van Buren's third point of criticism effects a smooth transition to the further difficulties of empirically informative statement, and historic factuality.

"This problem of words leads to our third objection: the kerygma of the New Testament contains statements which are empirical as well as some that are plainly existential, but its typical statements are mixed and their empirical aspect cannot logically be ignored." According to Bultmann, however, the statements of Christian faith and those of the kerygma are wholly existential: their function is not to inform, but to call the hearer to "self-understanding," and they are not subject to verification or proof. For van Buren, on the other hand, "the New Testament proclamation contains primarily statements whose logic is at least partly empirical."

He returns to the example of John 1:14: "The Word became flesh and dwelt among us." As van Buren comments, this statement "seems to be telling a fact, whatever other function it may have." This does not imply, of course, that van Buren is arguing against Bultmann for the "reality" or "historic factuality" of the incarnation. His point of criticism here is rather that the *appearance* of being a factual statement, and the logical structure of factual statement that gives rise to the appearance, have to be taken into account, and Bultmann has failed to do so. Bultmann insists that such phrases have to be demythologized: their purpose is to force the hearer to face the question of his own existence. Van Buren admits that they at least have to be reinterpreted. (We have already seen how he would go about this relying on contemporary biblical theology and the concept of "call" and "response." And in his seventh chapter, he further develops an exclusively secularist reading of the pertinent verse from John.) Van Buren likewise admits the existential purpose. But the summons of self-understanding is attached to an empirical declaration—of *some* sort. For "these statements do urge the reader to answer a question about himself and his relation to the world; but they seem also to give information, suggesting an appropriate response to the state of affairs described."

The example of Jesus' resurrection from the dead will help to clarify. In the resurrection proclamation, there is certainly a call to action. But the call to action is concretely dependent upon the hearer's being informed that something rendering such action appropriate has actually happened. For van Buren, as we

THE BREAK FROM TRADITION

saw earlier, what happened did not happen to Jesus, but to the disciples. And we noted that this interpretation, when intended exclusively, fails to do justice to the text. In principle, however, van Buren is certainly correct in observing against Bultmann that the attempt simply to ignore the empirical element in the Gospel statements is no solution to the problem which this element presents.

Van Buren's fourth point of criticism takes up the extremely important question of the historical Jesus. Just as the existentialist Left turns seemingly empirical statement into exclusively existential statement, so also does it turn seemingly historical event into "event" of some wholly different order. Thus van Buren quotes Ogden's quite categorical assertion that " 'the New Testament speaks of the cross as "the eschatological event", which never becomes an event in the past, but rather is constantly present both in preaching and sacraments . . . and in the believer's way of conducting his life'."

Van Buren, however, is very little impressed by this manner of speaking, and it is not at all because he has failed to appreciate the valid, even profound, insight which it nevertheless manifests. There is indeed more to the crucifixion than an event in the distant past. On the other hand, it was at least that; and it was certainly at least that for the New Testament writers. To try to circumvent this obviosity would be absurdity. At the moment, van Buren is thinking about the absurdity of the linguistic gymnastics which have to be employed. In the larger context of his overall critique, however, he sees the attempt to displace "the historical event of Jesus of Nazareth by the existential response of the believer" as removing from Christianity the only empirical base which it possesses.

In the same connection, to move on to van Buren's fifth and final criticism, the existentialist Left seeks to define the relationship of faith to Jesus of Nazareth without including the indispensable significance of Easter. Neither Bultmann nor

Ogden, but the latter especially, makes the role of Easter decisive. For Bultmann, the historical event was the beginning of faith in the disciples linked in some fashion to a sort of visionary experience. But Bultmann also implies that this beginning was also a renewal. Ogden is more explicit. For Ogden, "the issue had become sharper for the disciples as a result of Jesus' death, but the nature of faith, and that in which faith rested, remained unchanged. It is not surprising, therefore, that the resurrection plays no central part in his suggested solution of 'Christ without myth'."

In the judgment of the present writer, van Buren's criticism of the existentialist Left on the matter of its excessive and uncritical break with the historical Jesus of Nazareth may be in need of little further comment. For the Bultmannian exaggeration, or oversimplification, in this regard is coming more and more to be recognized as such in contemporary Christian theology—including many of the later Bultmannians. This is said, of course, on the supposition that what one desires to preserve and reinterpret of Christianity is to remain biblically grounded and biblically oriented. Admittedly, it is otherwise when, as perhaps in the case of Ogden, one's basic stance is what van Buren calls *theo*logical, and not *Christ*ological—and in this sense not really biblical—to begin with.

Before leaving the Bultmann question, however, the writer would like to offer at least one suggestion. Van Buren, as we have remarked from time to time, tends to take more or less for granted what he would consider Bultmann's positive contribution. But he does not come right out and say as much, and this leaves an impression that is probably more onesided than van Buren himself intends. For almost everything which he criticizes explicitly is criticized negatively, often even harshly so.

In any case, modern Christian theology owes a truly tremendous debt of gratitude to Rudolf Bultmann, and this will be observed more, not less, as the years go on, for the very good

reason that a number of theologians and exegetes—preoccupied less with the forest than with the trees—have not yet faced up to the essential Bultmannian challenge. Biblical criticism of the nineteenth century, and continued into the twentieth, saw with ever increasing clarity how it could determine, at least in principle, the "then and there" meaning immediate to the ancient text. But this was only half of the problem. Christian theology, as Christian faith, required that the "then and there" meaning be focussed also as the "here and now" meaning. For some, this posed no difficulty. The two are the same. Bultmann, however, recognized that they are not the same. Twentieth-century man is simply not first or second-century man. Hence, some sort of transposition is necessary; hence again, awareness of some sort of ultimate constant—whether or not one would seek to articulate this through the vehicle of existentialist categories. The theologian must first read the text, and read it so far as possible precisely the way it was written. But he cannot merely read the text, no matter how critically—not and go on talking glibly of its here and now message. As a matter of fact, no theologian really does. An automatic and sub-critical transposition is always at work. Bultmann's insight, however, was the method whereby it could be given scientifically critical form. The value of that insight considerably outbalances whatever was wanting, or is thought to have been wanting, in the details of its implementation. Also, as we shall want to observe in our critique of van Buren at the end of this chapter, his castigation of the Bultmann–Ogden notion of what we can call the non-empirical experience of the transcendent sounds extremely impressive in the context of rigidly empiricist presuppositions; outside the context of such presuppositions, however, but nevertheless within the context of strictly contemporary and even radical, patterns of thought, it sounds a great deal less so.

In any event, van Buren's fourth chapter immediately following, and entitled "Analyses of Theological Language," brings us

at least to the systematic discussion of what he has been telling us all along is the truly ultimate problem for religion, and for Christianity: What can we possibly mean when we say "God"? His criticism of the existentialist Left has set the stage. In a sense, and despite the range of van Buren's unfavorable observations, the existentialist Left is still the modern theology that, as it were, came closest to the goal. Its attempt was to render the Gospel intellectually and scientifically palatable. Its accomplishment was to reduce at least the myth. Bonhoeffer, it is true, had a better suggestion, but up until the new radical theology that suggestion was not acted upon.

It is largely, therefore, in the context of Christian Existentialism's retention of the idiom of transcendence, that van Buren passes on now to consider the contribution of the linguistic analysts. That is also why we postponed to this final section any more than incidental comment of our own upon van Buren's criticism of this particular point in the Bultmannian theology.

In recent times, van Buren begins, there has actually been an effort, mostly in and about the existentialist left, to define religion, and to show that Christianity is not exactly the same thing. Thus, "Bultmann defines religion as the human longing to escape from this world, fed by the supposed discovery of 'a sphere above this world, in which the soul alone, released from all that is worldly, could repose'." Van Buren concedes that most people would, in fact, consider such a longing and discovery religious. But there are many individuals who partake in religious activities, even go to church, and nevertheless show very little interest in the "sphere above." In van Buren's mind, "Bultmann's definition meets only one aspect of the problem which concerns us." Van Buren is much more attracted by Gerhard Ebeling's definition, echoing Bonhoeffer, as "the attempted 'enlargement of reality by means of God.' Religion consists of appealing to God as a means of explaining, justifying,

or otherwise 'filling in the picture' of the world or human affairs."

And this is precisely what contemporary theologians "from Barth to Ogden" insist that Christianity is not. "Religion, they would say, is man's use of God to solve some human problem, whereas the Gospel proclaims God's unexpected use of man for his own purposes; this distinction lies behind Bonhoeffer's search for a 'nonreligious' interpretation of biblical concepts." For van Buren, however, the distinction does not take us very far. The real problem is that all of these theologians are still talking about God. Ebeling at least recognizes this, plus the fact that large numbers today have no idea what such theological talk can possibly be about. But Ebeling himself, in van Buren's judgment, offers no effective substitute.

Now van Buren is equivalently dismissing an objection here. Up to this juncture, he has examined modern biblical theology in general, and the existentialist biblical theology in particular. The contribution of the former is modest, that of the latter somewhat more important but ultimately inadequate. It could be objected, however, that van Buren's critique has not done justice to a very significant element in the Bultmannian and neo-Bultmannian analysis. For under the pressure of debate, has not that analysis actually pushed beyond the immediate problems of myth and hermeneutic to take up the basic question of what it would mean to believe in God in the first place? Van Buren, however, both notes the fact and continues to stand his ground. The supposition even in the further, and in this sense philosophical, investigation remains that, whatever else we do, we at least have to go on talking about God. The truly basic question, therefore, is not posed at all.

Yet, and as van Buren realizes, the objection must be allowed one last turn. The existentialist theology does insist that we have to go on talking about God, but it does not do so uncritically; and this is just another way of saying that it has actually faced up to van Buren's problem, and has, moreover, given its own solution. As van Buren himself expresses it, "the solution proposed by existentialist theologians consists of eliminating all 'objectification' of God in thought and word." The problem in "the talk about God" is simply the problem of "objectification." Just as the Christian myth gave concrete form to the call to self-understanding by projecting "other-worldly things" such as incarnation and miraculous birth, so likewise did the Christian myth project a similarly "objectified" God. This means that the talk about God has to be radically corrected, and that objectification has to be eliminated.

On the final round, then, van Buren is confronted with the existentialist argument for a "non-objective" use of the word "God." His reply, however, is quite emphatic. He finds this kind of talk utterly meaningless. It would be otherwise if Bultmann allowed us to use the word "God" simply as a symbol for human experience. For such a use would be subject to verification. But Bultmann explicitly rejects this. On the one hand, therefore, the word does not stand for merely human experience; on the other, it is nonetheless non-objective. In van Buren's judgment, this leaves the word "God" no other fate than the death of a thousand qualifications. When all is said and done, Bultmann and Ebeling "continue to use the word 'God' as though it had a quite specific reference." By what logic, van Buren does not know.

With that, he turns to the linguistic analysts. The solution offered by the existentialist Left serves merely to aggravate the difficulty. "The problem of the Gospel in a secular age is a problem of the logic of its apparently meaningless language, and linguistic analysts will give us help in clarifying it."

We should note carefully the way van Buren expresses himself: "linguistic analysts will give us help in clarifying it." As we remarked previously, the heart of van Buren's argument is an appeal to the "empiricist attitudes" of contemporary secular society. Hence, the linguistic analysts whom he is about to introduce will not be giving him principles for deductive application, but simply a structure to assist him in articulating the empiricist presupposition. But empiricist presupposition is itself misleading. Van Buren's presupposition is more factual than doctrinal in kind. His explicit intention is not to ally himself with some empiricist dogma and then to work his way in the context of such a dogma's accepted theses, but rather to identify himself effectively with the empiricist "form" which represents the latest creative achievement in the evolution of modern secularized culture. If we asked him to footnote this last, he would probably tell us just to look out the window.

As van Buren puts it himself, he "set out upon this study with certain acknowledged commitments to what [he] called 'secular thought', and [he] said that secularism, as [he was] using the term, is grounded in empirical attitudes in some way." This is quite different from saying that he is approaching his subject matter as a dedicated Thomist or Kantian, or even, in the ordinary use of such terms, as a rationalist, a pragmatist, or an existentialist. Van Buren's self-categorization is much broader and much more neutral, so to speak. It is almost as though he were saying that he was simply trying to think and speak like an intelligent and educated man in the present-day Western, especially Anglo-Saxon, world. The empirical attitudes which he finds to be characteristic of such a man he also considers to be more common today, even among believers, than Bultmann or Ebeling seem to recognize. And this last remark, though it has heightened significance for the Anglo-Saxon community, is nevertheless clearly intended to embrace more than that community.

It is in this same broad and nonpartisan context, that van Buren states his fundamental position on the talk about God: "The empiricist in us [and by implication, the empiricist in anybody else] finds the heart of the difficulty not in what is said about God, but in the very talking about God at all. We do not know 'what' God is, and we cannot understand how the word 'God' is being used. It seems to function as a name, yet theologians tell us that we cannot use it as we do other names, to refer to something quite specific. If it is meant to refer to an 'existential encounter', a point of view, or the speaker's self-understanding, surely a more appropriate expression could be found. The problem is not solved, moreover, by substituting other words for the word *God:* one could supply the letter X . . . and the problem would remain, for the difficulty has to do with how X functions." And so van Buren takes his departure from the existentialist Left to turn to the linguistic analysts.

As van Buren reads the more recent history of linguistic analysis, and judges this history from the point of view of the relationship between linguistic analysis and theology, a significant development can be observed in what concerns the principle of verification. Earlier, the verification principle had required that only two types of statements could so much as be tested for meaningfulness: the intrinsically necessary statements of logic and mathematics on the one hand, and *empirically* verifiable statements on the other. But religious statements quite obviously do not belong to the first class; and only a limited number of religious statements would belong to the second: for empirical verification, as here understood, presupposes the order of the strictly factual and the context of sense and sensory experience, whereas very many religious statements, and ultimately the more crucial ones, presuppose, at least on face value, precisely the opposite. In its earlier and stricter form, therefore, the verification principle would be of little positive assistance to the theology of the language of faith.

More recently, however, linguistic analysis has revised the verification principle to take account of several possible "language games" in which words and statements may be used. Thus, the meaningfulness of a given statement reduces, in the last inspection, to its linguistic "function": does it actually achieve anything serious in the line of human communication, and if so, of what nature? But in this now widened context, van Buren observes, religious statements are quite verifiable. They do have a demonstrable communicative function, a communicative function, moreover, which the empirically minded modern man is perfectly capable of recognizing and managing. To bring this out, van Buren examines—but rather briefly, it should be noted—the pertinent reflections of four well-known contemporary linguistic analysts. Once again, however, it is necessary to make clear that the purpose of the examination is not to present to us the philosophy which van Buren has appropriated, or even the philosophy which he has used as the point of departure for his own ideas. The purpose is rather the much more limited one of making us acquainted with a small group of scholars who evidently share van Buren's already existing basic attitudes, and have helped him to some extent to give to these attitudes a more systematic expression.

Thus, R. M. Hare has called attention to the difference between statements which depend upon empirical inquiry, and statements which clearly do not, but serve rather to declare one's fundamental attitudes or basic presuppositions about the world and human existence. Such an attitude or presupposition, Hare calls a "*blik*." Statements involving a "*blik*" are not, at least in the stricter application, empirically verifiable. On the other hand, they do make sense: they have a distinct and positive function. For instance, the statement "God loves all men" cannot be tested for meaningfulness so long as it is taken to signify "how things are," but it can be tested for meaningfulness when it is seen as a declaration of the believer's personal "orientation, a commitment to see the world in a certain way, and a way of life following inevitably upon this orientation." As Van Buren concludes, "what Hare is suggesting is that a man's faith and his theology have a meaning, even though the theistic rug has been pulled out from under him."

We will recall, however, that if van Buren himself is convinced of anything it is the necessity of centering Christianity in the historical reality of Jesus of Nazareth, and hence in the empirical statements of fact which mediate that historical reality. True, there comes a point at which religious utterances no longer give factual information, yet nevertheless continue to communicate seriously. Hare's suggestion of the "*blik*" is valuable, therefore. But it addresses itself to only one half of the total problem: the "*blik*," the orientation, the commitment to a way of life, has still to be related to the empirical statements of fact which at least appear to provide its genetic context.

This brings van Buren to the contribution of another prominent linguistic analyst, Ian T. Ramsey. When Ramsey's "analysis is applied to the language of Christology," to take this highly significant concrete instance, "it discloses two sorts of languages: one is the language of a "*blik*"; the other is that of straightforward empirical observation." But the two are genetically related. For in Ramsey's mind, the statements of faith exhibit a twofold aspect. Ultimately, their function is to announce an extremely special kind of "disconcernment" which has produced in the believer an accompanying "commitment" henceforth to view the world and live his life in a new and special way. The discernment-commitment so expressed, however, is related to the basic "situation" which came to "disclose" itself in such "depth." For "statements of faith direct our attention to certain kinds of situations: situations of disclosure, when 'the light dawns', and the situation becomes alive and new." At an earlier moment, therefore, and so to speak, the same statements of faith serve to make available at the quite factual level that which will be the focal point of the eventual discernment. Thus it is that the language of Christology is twofold: again, that of the "*blik*," and that of the straightforward empirical observation. "Both sorts of language are used about the same person, Jesus of Nazareth. But the language of Christology is appropriate only to one who himself has discerned what Christians discern, for whom Jesus has become the occasion for a new discernment which has led to a commitment involving his whole perspective. We can summarize by saying that the language of Christology is language about Jesus of Nazareth on the part of those for whom he has been the occasion and remains the definition of their "*blik*." The "he," however, is the Jesus of Nazareth who has been, and as he has been, described empirically in the New Testament.

Van Buren cites with enthusiasm Ramsey's approach to the language of the resurrection. On the one hand, there are the observable factors: the empty tomb and the resuscitated body. "What the Christian believes about the resurrection of Jesus has something to do with these observable factors, but it is not identical with them." For in Ramsey's mind, one could acknowledge the observable factors and still not become a believer. Hence, for the true believer, resurrection means a great deal more: "the word 'resurrection' (like the words 'duty', 'love', and 'God') directs us to the sort of situation in which a discernment fundamental to our whole conception of life and a response of commitment may take place. Such situations exceed empirical description, however relevant description may be to our discernment." Earlier in the present study, when we were discussing the question of van Buren's apparent atheism, we saw how he himself would then go ahead to interpret the Easter event in much the same spirit as Ramsey. The situation is the life and death of the historical Jesus of Nazareth. As this life and death discloses itself to the Christian believer, he discerns in it Jesus' unique freedom, catches its powerful contagion, and commits himself irrevocably to the style of life which this discernment demands.

Next, van Buren notes that T. R. Miles likewise has performed an analysis of the language of faith that is similar to those of Hare and Ramsey. The treatment of Miles' contribution, however, is much more summary.

Finally, van Buren comes to the work of R. B. Braithwaite, which he considers more important than that of any of the others for his own study. According to Braithwaite, religious or theological propositions cannot possibly be, in the stricter or factual sense, empirical. For the laws of verification require that one determine, as the primary question, not whether or not the statement "God created the world" is true or false, but rather how such a statement could be known to be true or false. To rule, therefore, that the statement "God created the world" is an empirical statement of fact, one would have to be able to indicate how the world or the course of history would have been different without God, or one would have to grant that if either had been different we could conclude that there is no God.

If such statements, then, cannot possibly be empirical statements of fact, what is their value? For Braithwaite, the key to the mystery lies simply in this: "religious assertions are in fact *used as* moral assertions." The moral assertion too is neither logically necessary nor empirical; but it does have a use: to guide conduct. "With the significant modification which has been made in the early verification principle (so that philosophers would now say that 'the meaning of a statement is given by the way in which it is used'), it is now realized that 'the primary use of a moral assertion [is] that of expressing the intention of the asserter to act in a particular sort of way specified in the assertion'." But religious assertions also are " 'primarily declarations of adherence to a policy of action, declarations of commitment to a way of life.' " And Braithwaite goes further: " 'the intention of a Christian to follow a Christian way of life is not only the criterion for the sincerity of his belief in the assertions of Christianity; it is the criterion for the meaningfulness of his assertions. Just as the meaning of a moral assertion is given by its use in expressing the asserter's intention to act, so far as in him lies, in accordance with the moral principle involved, so the meaning of a religious assertion is given by its use in expressing the asserter's intention to follow a specified policy of behaviour'."

If it is objected that not all religious statements imply action, Braithwaite will counter that the statements of Christianity must be taken in their ensemble and in context. A more serious objection, however, and broadly similar to the one that had to be faced by Ramsey, would demand that the statement interpreted as expressing the asserter's intention to act be related to, and somehow integrated with, the statements which have to be interpreted as at least seeming to imply factual content. And here Braithwaite distinguishes between religion and morality: " 'a religious assertion will . . . have a propositional element which is lacking in a purely moral assertion, in that it will refer to a story as well as to an intention'. Consequently, 'to assert the whole set of assertions of the Christian religion is both to tell the Christian doctrinal story and to confess allegiance to the Christian way of life'. . . . The Christian story includes straight history and also material clearly not historical. But Braithwaite insists that belief in the empirical truth of the stories 'is not the proper criterion for deciding whether or not an assertion is a Christian one. A man is not, I think, a professing Christian unless he both proposes to live according to Christian moral principles and associates his intention with thinking of Christian stories; but he need not believe that the empirical propositions presented by the stories correspond to empirical fact'."

When further pressed as to the more exact function of the story, Braithwaite offers an explanation that is more or less exclusively psychological. Thus, "to say that an action is 'doing the will of God' helps to carry it through." But van Buren considers this explanation the one possible weak spot in the entire analysis. And it should be noted at this juncture that if van Buren's Gospel reinterpretation owes something by way of suggestion and precision to the British linguistic analysts, it also departs from them in making much more simple and incisive the by-play between the factually empirical and the religious. For Ramsey and Braithwaite, there seem to be three distinct elements: first, the statement of fact or at least which seems to be that; secondly, the more or less exclusively psychological value which has to be set upon the seeming statement of fact; thirdly and finally, the *"blik,"* or discernment, or intention to act, as declared by the non-empirical statements of Christian faith. For van Buren himself, on the other hand, there are only two elements: first, the statement of fact, and which is to be taken as such in utter seriousness: the birth, something of the life and personality, and the death of the historical Jesus of Nazareth; secondly, the non-empirical statement of Christian faith which must be secularized, and hence interpreted in at least the general direction of the *"blik,"* or discernment, or intention to act, but always in immediate and strictly causal relation to the historical Jesus of Nazareth.

We should not be surprised, therefore, at the reserve with which van Buren concludes his brief survey (even calling it that) of the linguistic analysts. "Our brief survey of several attempts to interpret the language of faith by means of linguistic analysis does not of itself give us a method for our reconstructive task. It does suggest, however, a basis for understanding the language of faith which can be applied to the biblical and patristic assertions concerning Jesus of Nazareth, but only a short section in one of Ramsey's books gives even a hint of what such an interpretation of the Gospel might be." And it is precisely the Gospel that van Buren must reinterpret; whereas, he adds, most of the examples of the language of faith cited by the linguistic analysts belong rather to what has been called natural theology.

The detail of the reinterpretation, however, and aside from what we saw of it in the preceding chapter, need not detain us. For the heart of the project is quite clearly what van Buren does with the historical Jesus and Easter. Everything else depends upon this, and is controlled by it. And what van Buren does with Jesus and Easter is simply to avoid God. His reason for excluding God, moreover, has not really been taken from the linguistic analysts. The speculations of Hare, Ramsey and Braithwaite have helped him to see how one might give an exclusively empirical interpretation to Jesus and to Easter *if one had to*. There would still remain the "*blik*," the discernment, the intention to act; for these were always there, and it is the insight of the linguistic analysts to have perceived their presence in the complex language of faith. But the fact that one *does have to* work out such an exclusively empirical interpretation, this was van Buren's own conviction from the beginning. As he told us himself, the empiricist in him, and by implication in anyone else who really belongs to the world of today, can no longer talk about "God." For it is impossible to use the word empirically; and the attempts, chiefly that of the existentialist Left, to use either the word or one of its many substitutes in some non-empirical or extended way leads only to absurdities. In the final analysis, therefore, the crux of van Buren's whole argument can be expressed in two consecutive propositions: first, it is impossible to talk empirically about God; secondly, and the man of today must always talk empirically.

Now we are not going to challenge in the least van Buren's first point: that we cannot talk empirically about God at all. Nor are we going to dispute with van Buren over the *de facto* "empirical-mindedness" of today's scientific and secular man. But we do suggest that modern man's "empirical-mindedness" is not his "total-mindedness," and that the footnote for this too is look out the window.

What is at issue here is the scope of human experience. In two passages previously cited, van Buren leaves not the slightest residue of doubt as to what he personally considers that scope to be. First, he demolishes Ogden's expression "experienced nonobjective reality" by noting that the word "experience" is ordinarily used for what can in some way be sensed. And it is frequently reiterated throughout van Buren's study, at least by unmistakable implication, that the ordinary use of words is the only permissible use, in theology as everywhere else. Secondly, in his reconstruction of the Easter event he argues with emphasis that Easter, whatever it was, could not have been "merely a subjective experience." For an experience, any experience, is always an experience *of* something. And the *of,* as van Buren's reductionist exegesis of the Easter narrative demonstrates, is always to be understood as *of* what can in some way be sensed.

For van Buren, then, the scope of human experience is the scope of sense. Or to put it another way, every human experience is ultimately empirical. In one place, it is true, van Buren allows that certain of the Gospel statements must be taken existentially, others empirically. But the force of his distinction here is not to admit the non-empirical, or trans-empirical, into the ambient of human experience. It is simply to observe that some statements inform, while others call to action. Both the call and the response, however, are to be interpreted empirically. In short, therefore, van Buren's network of value equivalents combines experience, object *of* experience, something of sense, and something empirical into a single closed circuit.

Now for some, this would be the place to remind van Buren (or at least our readers) of the difference between sense and intellect, and of the truth of human spirituality which can be concluded from that difference. But this would not be an answer to van Buren's question. For in our view there is no such thing —in academic dialogue—as an *answer* which is not an answer to the *question* precisely. There may, of course, be a *solution,* but a solution is something else.

The *philosophia perennis* addresses itself to the problem of the scope of human experience, and solves it in its own fashion. The solution begins from an analysis of man's psychological operations, and argues to an order of intellect distinct from that of sense, and then to an order of spirit distinct from that of matter. The writer himself, as it happens, considers that solution valid; and he has no objection to discussing it with those who are not unwilling to accept its style. But van Buren, quite obviously, is not among them. Nor is this all. Van Buren has his own style, and he has gone to the scholar's trouble of presenting in that style a carefully reasoned case. For our part, we would prefer to stick to the text of that case. We would be quite adverse to superimposing upon the conversation an idiom and a pattern of analysis that has nothing to do with van Buren's on the one hand, while ignoring van Buren's own on the other.

We shall keep, then, to the text. And we suggest that there is in the text itself a single, but extremely important, weakness. It is not in van Buren's insistence that modern man is "empirically minded." For when stated positively, and not also exclusively, that is certainly true. But van Buren's assertion is, in fact, exclusively intended, and the immediate reason for this lies in what accompanies his understanding of human experience as always and necessarily experience *of.*

In van Buren's view, any something of which we have experience, the full spectrum of somethings of which we have experience, is, like experience itself, empirical, and at least in some way a matter of sense. We do not, therefore, have experience of "nonobjective reality," or of "the transcendent," or of "the absolute," or of "the ground and end of all things." The most we can do is form ideas of such "things," and then attempt to indicate what we mean. But the attempt is doomed to failure, because there is no language on earth which can both convey the content of such ideas and still pass the test for meaningful utterance.

Van Buren, however, seems to overlook something that is rather consistently reported of human experience. Modern scientific and secular man continues to talk every now and then of the moments in his experience when there is a blank after the *of:* experience of _____. He speaks, for example, of a "moment of awareness," a "moment of communication," a "moment of discernment" perhaps, or even a "moment of mystery." Words are added after the *of:* "awareness," "communion," "discernment," "mystery." The blank is actually filled in on paper and in speech. But this is deceptive. For these words do not seem to stand for the object of the experience at all. Rather, they seem to double back simply on the word "experience," calling attention in some perhaps obscure way to its shape, or tone, or quality, at the purely subjective or personal level. The blank after the *of,* therefore, remains precisely a blank. Yet, as van Buren notes, every human experience is still experience *of* something. So the blank has to be retained even though it cannot be filled in with something determinate at the objective level.

Van Buren, not improbably, would want to ask at this point whether we were not merely bringing back into the conversation just another "God substitute." To the already overdrawn list—"nonobjective reality," "transcendent," "absolute," "ground and end of all things"—we now add "the indeterminate" or "the _____"! We would reply, however, that this is not our intention. The "God substitutes" try to define the object of religious experience without objectification of the projected sort, or the sort that is associated with myth-making. When all is said and done, they fill in the blank. We wish rather to leave it a blank.

As a matter of fact, when modern man talks about his moments of awareness, or moments of mystery, or anything else of this nature, the writer does not personally believe that the content of the experience, or what follows the *of,* is actually what conventional theology has called the absolute—certainly not automatically, nor in the first instance. More likely, we feel, the experience being talked about, however obscurely, is the speaker's faint intuition of his own spiritual quality: the heightened awareness of consciousness, and the activation of subjectivity, that accompanies the more precious moments of understanding, decision and responsible personal commitment. Sometimes the individual leaves it at such a heightened awareness, and sometimes he attempts to bring it, as he does any other experience, into touch with his own critical faculties. He may, for example, take up the study of oriental mysticism, to see if he can find some clue as to what he has been experiencing. Eventually, to be sure, he may come to discover the transcendent sacred and what he believes to be God. But we by no means want to argue that he has already done so, and quite automatically.

Our answer to van Buren here is modest and restricted. We are simply playing porter. Van Buren wants to slam the door once and for all: the empiricist can no longer recognize as pertaining to the scope of human experience whatever would not be, on the hypothesis of the case, experience *of* something, and *of* something sensible; nor, by the same token, can the empiricist any longer tolerate the attempts of language to give articulate form to such counterfeit experience. But we submit that if van Buren's real intention is to say simply that no intelligent and educated modern man can do this, it is just not factually correct—not as it stands. For the typical empirically minded modern man does allow at least one exception to van Buren's rule, and in the nature of the situation that exception is decisive. He is frankly conscious of moments of experience, to this extent both empirical and sensible, in which, if and when he tries to describe the experience, nothing definite and sensible can be inserted after the *of*.

In our judgment, this is quite enough to leave open the door which van Buren wants to close. The empiricist will not talk outside the scope of human experience. This is true. But it is not true, on the other hand, that the empiricist will apodictically exclude from the legitimate scope of human experience that to which he cannot assign what is in principle a clearly defined sensed object.

Within very fixed limits, therefore, many empiricists, the writer suspects the majority, are not adverse to the notion of the sacred. It is not, of course, another name for God; and the one admitting its relevance for human existence might be an atheist. But it suggests some of the things that are in the back of the empiricist's mind when he reflects upon certain privileged but seemingly "objectless" moments in his personal experience. Cox, at this point, talks quite candidly even of the transcendent, though not, to be sure, in the sense of some "other-worldly" projection. And his criticism of van Buren is sharp. Cox believes "that van Buren is wrong when he states that modern, secular man does not experience the transcendent."

Van Buren, then, has overstated his case, and it is very important that we note the fact at just this juncture. For in the remaining pages of Part One and throughout Part Two, the entire movement of van Buren's thought is systematically controlled by the not quite valid factual assumption that the intelligent, empirically minded man of today does not recognize any other than van Buren's purely empirical experience. This, of course, by no means deprives the study of all positive value. Van Buren's Gospel reconstruction, even as a Gospel of Jesus from which God has been excluded, continues to be rich in theological insights. In our view, it could actually be said that the "Jesus-without-God" who emerges from the enquiry, "the man for others" in whom is realized the highest ideal of human freedom, may well be the only Jesus whom the modern empiricist could ever possibly accept someday as truly divine. But this is looking to the future. It is not at all the point which van Buren himself is here and now trying to make. For van Buren, "Jesus-without-God" is the end of the road, and it is the empiricist assumption that forces this conclusion.

Now we have remarked already that van Buren is a neat and consistent writer. In the key section of the book which we are now considering, however, it does seem that the author's mind might have been expressed more clearly, and that as things now stand, a reader could come away without appreciating the full extent to which the empiricist assumption governs the whole argument.

First, we cannot talk empirically about God. Now this much is perfectly clear; and as we have observed, it is also incontestable. Therefore, van Buren goes on, the "God-statements" in the Gospel cannot be taken as empirical statements of fact. That "the Word became flesh," if intended as an empirical statement of fact, is an utterance that could never be verified. This is likewise clear, and likewise incontestable. For van Buren means that it could never be verified empirically, and in an extremely technical sense of empirical verification. But if the utterance "the Word became flesh" is not intended as an empirical statement of fact, is it not, for all that, a straightforward affirmation of what we believe, as Christians, to be literally true? To this further question, of course, the vast majority of Christian theologians will say yes. Does van Buren himself, however, say no? But this is what is not immediately clear.

Actually, and as we saw when treating van Buren's reinterpretation of the Easter event, his reply to the further question, the question of simple truth and objective reality, is a plea for silence. For in van Buren's mind, there is no way in which we could possibly establish either the yes or the no. The empiricist can admit no other language than the empirical, and in empirical language "God-statements" have no assignable meaning.

Yet, in the section now under consideration, the all-important final pages of Part One, is not van Buren's point precisely the opposite? The argument seems to move as follows: We cannot talk empirically about God; therefore, the "God-statements," such as "the Word became flesh," must be interpreted in another, presumably non-empirical, way. Moreover, this other, non-empirical way is spelled out. What has the linguistic form of an empirical statement of fact, "the Word became flesh," is really the declaration of a certain "*blik*," or discernment, or intention to act, on the part of the believer. It is the believer's way of saying that henceforth, so to speak, his over-all approach to life, reality and the world about him will be radically conditioned by this new perspective.

In the final analysis, therefore, and despite everything he asserts to the contrary, does not van Buren admit into religious discourse other than strictly empirical language? The conclusion, however, is misleading. Implicit in van Buren's argument, and saving it from contradiction at a very critical moment, is a distinction between a strict and somewhat broader form of nevertheless empirical language. The strict form, perhaps we could call it "empiricality of the first order," is the empirical statement of fact: Jesus of Nazareth was crucified in such a place at such a time. Of the same strict form, would *appear* to be also this further statement: "the Word was made flesh." For at least in its superficial linguistic structure, it too looks like an empirical statement of fact. On examination, however, we perceive that it cannot possibly be intended as such. For how could we ever authenticate, or verify, an empirical statement of fact about a divine Word? About God? So the second statement has to be interpreted differently. It is not an empirical statement of fact at all.

Hence, van Buren does try to interpret it differently. Thus, he admits something other than the first and stricter form of empirical language. He even goes so far as to refer explicitly to the believer's *"blik"* as non-empirical, while making the *"blik"* at the same time the actually essential element in his now thoroughly meaningful reinterpretation. But van Buren means only that the *"blik"* or the discernment, or the intention to act, is not empirical in the stricter sense. For if, on the one hand, it is not an empirical statement of fact, it remains, on the other, a personal experience which should in no way embarrass even the man-eating empiricist. In a slightly broader sense of the word, it is still empirical. In the final paragraph of Part One, though the reader may wish that he had not waited so long, van Buren himself makes this point clear. "These remarks," he writes, "on a method of analyzing theological statements reveal that we share certain empirical attitudes with some linguistic analysts. We have not said how far these attitudes take us nor to what degree they are shared, and our use of the word 'empirical' has therefore been somewhat loose. It is clear that we have little difficulty with the statement that John is heavier than Jane, and we are reasonably sure of the empirical footing of this assertion. Do we want to say that 'John loves Jane' is empirical? We certainly want to say that it is a comprehensible and meaningful statement in a 'secular' age, and that this is because it meets certain empirical expectations which we have upon hearing statements about human activities and relationships. But we should also want to say that the empirical commitments of what we have loosely called secularism do not exclude our saying that there is a difference between my saying 'John loves Jane' and John saying 'I love Jane'. The empirical attitudes of secularism, as we are using the term, have room also for this third statement." When all is said and done, therefore, van Buren's "secular meaning of the Gospel" is empiricist, and intentionally so, throughout.

To conclude, then, the message of *The Secular Meaning of*

the Gospel reduces, as we have already observed, to the following compound proposition: we cannot talk empirically about God; but we must always talk empirically—or else, he adds immediately, be silent. In attempting to refute van Buren, Mascall defended the notion of supernatural empirical events, and we noted that it would have been better had he simply conceded the point that we cannot talk empirically about supernatural events. Now Mascall is far too good a philosopher to want to defend as well a notion of God as empirical object. On the other hand, he does not seem to want to come right out and admit, with van Buren, that we cannot talk empirically about God. But it would be better if he conceded this further point also. For this, far from being the weak spot in van Buren's argument, is perfectly valid. The weak spot is rather in his insistence that we must always talk empirically, and in the reason he gives: as a matter of fact, modern empirically minded man can talk no other way. But the matter of fact here can be challenged.

What likewise can be challenged is the responsibility of van Buren's demand for absolute silence on the yes or no of God. Responsibility means a great deal to van Buren, and this is brought out in *The Christian Century* article already referred to even more than it had been in the book. His search is not for abstract truth, but rather to discover how present-day theology might best fulfill its obligation to cultural history. In such a context, however, and in the light of such a goal, absolute silence on the yes or no of God could be judged responsible only inasmuch as it had met rather harsh conditions. One of these would be the incontestable fact that in the course of cultural evolution modern empirically minded man had arrived at the stage where he could no longer talk in a way that made discussion of the yes or no of God even a possibility. But at the very least, van Buren would have to admit that this is not an incontestable fact at the present moment, for all that he might feel that it soon will be. For at the present moment, even his fellow radicals split on the point. The truly responsible stance, therefore, would certainly seem to be that of openness to further exploration rather than that of categorical resignation to absolute silence. Still another condition that would have to be met is the final removal from man's serious concern of the problem posed by the quite empirical fact of human death: extinction or immortality? For unless modern man confronts at least the possibility of immortality, it seems that his only realistic alternative is to accept the absurdity of human existence, human progress, human spirit, human creativity. And this is where van Buren could perhaps learn much from Bultmann and the existentialists.

Finally, there is the question of how faithful van Buren has been to the Bonhoeffer he promised he was going to follow. Bonhoeffer had written in paradox: "And we cannot be honest without recognizing that we must live in the world as though God were not [*Und wir können nicht redlich sein, ohne zu erkennen, dass wir in der Welt leben müssen—'etsi deus non daretur'*]." Now van Buren quotes Bonhoeffer accurately. In his opening paragraph, he retains the "*etsi deus non daretur*," rendering the Latin "as if there were no God." But from that moment on, he drops the paradox completely. God is henceforth systematically excluded. This, however, had not been Bonhoeffer's idea at all. For Bonhoeffer had not only spoken paradoxically about the mystery of having to live in the world "as though God did not exist," but continued to pray up until his final hour to the God he believed did exist.

Also, it should be mentioned here at least in passing that the key phrase as it appears in the Bonhoeffer original, or more precisely in Bethge's editing, presents a problem of correct interpretation and translation. Van Buren, as we just noted, does quote accurately the Latin words "*etsi deus non daretur*." But his translation makes it seem that he did not read them accurately: he renders the phrase "*as if* there were no God"; but "*etsi*" means "*even* if," not "*as* if." Thus Robinson translates the Latin as "even if God is not there'," which preserves the correct meaning of "*etsi*," but does not preserve the mood of the verb "*daretur*." Robinson should write "even if God *were* not 'there'," not "even if God *is* not 'there'."

Now there are a number of possibilities here, even if they do not affect in the least the really important conclusion that Bonhoeffer's non-existence challenge was intended paradoxically, since this is absolutely clear from other passages in the *Letters and Papers,* including the final paragraph of the same letter in which the "*etsi*" clause occurs. It is no less clear, in fact, from the immediate context of the "*etsi*" passage itself: however we are to conceive the withdrawal of God's presence and the negation of his existence, it is "before God!" that we are to do so.

The single line itself, however, does present a problem. As it stands, the German would have to be rendered: "And we cannot be honest unless we recognize that we have to live in the world—even if there were no God." One possibility is that this is exactly what Bonhoeffer wrote and exactly what he meant to write. Grammatically, the structure is abrupt: "We have to live in the world—even if there were no God." A correction suggests itself: "we *would* have to live in the world—even if there were no God." But this would alter the mood of the German verb "*müssen*," and do still greater violence to Bonhoeffer's theology and sense of logic. If, then, the phrase is to be left as it stands, it is probably elliptical: "we have to live in the world (*as we would have to*) even if God did not exist." And this would be simply another way of stating Bonhoeffer's proposition that we have to live in the world without "the God hypothesis," that in a profound, but paradoxical, sense we have to assume exclusive responsibility for our own existence and welfare.

It is also possible, however, that just as van Buren saw "*etsi*" (*even* if) in the text, but, as it seems, thought "*ac si*" (*as* if),

Bonhoeffer himself wrote *"etsi,"* but thought *"ac si."* If this is true, it simplifies things considerably. But the net result is unchanged in the least: we are being challenged, by God himself, to live in the world without "the God hypothesis."

Paul van Buren, then, to resume our main theme, belongs to the Secularization movement to the extent that he focusses sharply upon the basic problem of talking about God in a rapidly secularizing world. For this reason, it is important to consider his contribution. But what makes it still more important is the necessity of showing even at some length that van Buren's ultimately apodictic exclusion of God in his attempt to offer a solution to the basic problem is neither critically justified in itself, nor actually representative of either Bonhoeffer's own thought, or of those others who have tried to give form to that Secularized Christianity which is faithful to the true meaning and implications of Bonhoeffer's original challenge.

III.

The Creative Insights

A MOMENT AGO, we remarked that, while van Buren has not really contributed in our judgment to the positive development of the Bonhoeffer Secularized Christianity, he has nevertheless focussed sharply upon the basic problem of talking about God in present-day society. Right now, however, we shall be limiting our attention to what we consider to be the principal creative insights of the Bonhoeffer tradition, and this is not the area, if our judgment is correct, in which van Buren has very much to offer.

It seems, then, that we can turn immediately to the constructive theologizing of John Robinson and Harvey Cox. But should we not first, someone will ask, say something about Bonhoeffer himself?

Undoubtedly, we should, yet it is difficult to do so. For we are not here and now discussing Bonhoeffer's over-all theology, nor the evolution of his personal reflexions over a wide area, but only that aspect of his thinking which can be shown to have been the jumping-off point for the Secularization movement that today attaches itself to his name. But on this much more restricted topic we could add relatively little to what we had noted in the opening chapter. Van Buren took from Bonhoeffer two leads: the challenge to live in the world as though God did not exist, and the ideal of identification with the historical Jesus of Nazareth as "the man for others." On the other hand, what van Buren made of these two leads can hardly be assigned to Bonhoeffer. For van Buren dropped the paradox in the "*etsi deus non daretur*"; and his "man for others" became not only a thoroughly "worldly" Jesus of Nazareth, but a Jesus of Nazareth from whom God had been positively excluded. In point of fact, both Robinson and Cox also took the same two leads, without, however, either destroying the paradox in the challenge of God's "non-existence," or reducing true divinity in the ideal of "the man for others."

Yet, where the question of Bonhoeffer's role is concerned the remarks just made are most unsatisfactory. Without further elaboration, does not the "non-existence" paradox sound very much like rhetorical ruse, and the "man for others" ideal little more than pious slogan? By what right, moreover, could we say that one line of subsequent development was authentically Bonhoeffer, and another not, if the original stood almost entirely without explanation? If it is true, however, that Bonhoeffer wrote very little in expansion of his two central ideas, dying before he had any opportunity to set about such a task, it is not true that he failed to leave behind enough to make sufficiently clear at least the broad and general thrust of his intentions.

In Bonhoeffer's mind, then, we cannot be honest unless we recognize that God himself wants us to live in the world as though he did not exist. Now from the context of the same section in *Letters and Papers from Prison* in which this "non-existence" paradox is expressed, rather a number of things are clear. The challenge is a challenge to responsibility specifically; it blueprints the only possible religious attitude of the man who has truly come of age in a world that has come of age. Further, the God who no longer exists, and who is telling us that he no longer exists, is defined from two closely related points of view, and two points of view which are directly related to mature human responsibility, both intellectual and moral. First, the God who no longer exists is the God who is constantly intervening in the affairs of men. But the intervening which Bonhoeffer is thinking about is that which traditional theology would call, not supernatural, but, as explained in our first chapter, preternatural. And the positive point which Bonhoeffer wants to make here is that in this context of the marvel God's ordinary way of dealing with the world is to leave what traditional theology calls secondary causes to themselves. This does not mean leaving them without God: the only reason secondary causes are called secondary is that the operation of the primary cause, God, is thereby explicitly accounted for. But it does mean leaving them without that which would be conceived as further intervention. Secondly, the God who no longer exists is the God who is "brought in"—a postulated hypothesis—either to fill in the intellectual and scientific gaps left open through human ignorance, or the moral gaps left open through human failure to assume proper and full responsibility. This is the God that *God* is telling us no longer exists. The paradox is not at all frivolous: it expresses, in fact, what is a perfectly valid, and possibly profound, theological insight.

Another question that could be asked here is whether or not the Bonhoeffer plea for a "religionless Christianity" was simply another way of expressing the "non-existence" paradox. For all practical purposes, yes. When Bonhoeffer defined the "religious perspective" as far back as the time when he was working on the *Ethics,* the "religiousness" that he was thinking of was precisely that which was based on intellectual naïveté and moral irresponsibility. And in *Letters and Papers from Prison,* in the same letter and only a few lines after he had written that we must live in the world as though God did not exist, he linked the paradox to the "religionless" concept explicitly, and linked both to the extremely kenoticist Christology of his "man for others": "This is the decisive difference between Christianity and all religions. Man's religiosity makes him look in his distress to the power of God in the world; he uses God as a *deus ex machina*. The Bible however directs him to the powerlessness and suffering of God; only a suffering God can help. To this extent we may say that the process we have described by which the world came of age was an abandonment of a false conception of God, and a clearing of the decks for the God of the Bible, who conquers power and space in the world by his weakness. This must be the starting point for our 'worldly' interpretation."

But if Bonhoeffer's "non-existence" paradox was by no means merely theological rhetoric, neither was his "man for others" ideal merely pious slogan. Ultimately, the key to the content of the "man for others" conception is simply secularization. The remote biblical foundation for the conception goes all the way back to the Servant Songs in Deutero-Isaiah. Bonhoeffer's "man for others" is the Suffering Servant. But by itself, emphasis on the Suffering Servant motif, and on a consequently "functional" notion of the identity of Jesus, is not what is distinctive of Bonhoeffer. For it is shared by many others. We come closer to what is distinctive of Bonhoeffer, however, when we note the kenoticist element, or more accurately, since this by itself is likewise shared by many others, when we note that Bonhoeffer's kenoticism takes a precisely secularized turn. To the traditional Christian idea of the "self-emptying" of the Word's incarnation, Bonhoeffer adds the point that the Jesus of Nazareth so divested is the Jesus of a strictly secularized, or "religionless," Christianity: the Jesus freed once and for all from every false concept of respect for God. On the more positive side, it is also the Jesus in whom the man of today's secularized world can recognize the consummate instance of historical, social, political —in every sense, and best sense, "worldly"—responsibility.

The detail, then, is still scanty, but even such as it is, it is theologically significant. We have here, moreover, the Bonhoeffer who was the main inspiration behind *Honest to God,* and in all probability *The Secular City*—the latter, inasmuch as we should combine with the impressions left by the book Cox's more pointed analysis of the role of Bonhoeffer that first appeared as an article in *The Commonweal,* and has since been republished as a rejoinder in the volume entitled *The Secular City Debate* edited by Daniel Callahan.

Let us consider, then, and in greater detail than was possible in our introductory chapter, the truly constructive and creative, though perhaps not truly original, aspect of what Secularization means to Bishop John Robinson.

In *Honest to God,* the first two chapters are extremely negative. This is the demolishing and destructive stage of the undertaking, and "destructive" is exactly the word which Robinson himself uses to describe it. What he is concerned with here is what has to go: Christianity's way of conceiving God as "up there" or even "out there." More specifically, Christianity has got to stop being three things. With Tillich, it must stop being "supranaturalist." With Bultmann, it must stop being "mythological." And with Bonhoeffer, it must stop being "religious." At this point, moreover, Robinson is quite content to let Tillich, Bultmann and Bonhoeffer speak for themselves.

The next two chapters, in contrast, are positive. If something has to go, something different must be put in its place. There is still little or no originality: the something different will be that which had already been given to Christianity, for all that the gift went largely unappreciated, by Tillich and Bonhoeffer. But the suggestions Robinson now offers are at least constructive, certainly so in intention.

The first of these is that the contemporary Christian accept without reserve the Tillichian correction of divine transcendence. As was brought out in Tillich's biblical reflections to which Robinson will appeal a moment later, it is not the authentic spirit of the bible itself that man either look for God "up there" or think of him as "out there." Rather, "the man who acknowledges the transcendence of God is the man who *in* the conditioned relationships of life recognizes the unconditional and responds to it in unconditional personal relationship. In Tillich's words again, "To call God transcendent in this sense does not mean that one must establish a 'super-world' of divine objects. It does mean that, within itself, the finite world points beyond itself. In other words, it is self-transcendent'." Robinson adds immediately: "This, I believe, is Tillich's great contribution to theology—the reinterpretation of transcendence in a way which preserves its reality while detaching it from the projection of supranaturalism."

The second suggestion is that the contemporary Christian join to Tillich's reinterpretation of transcendence Bonhoeffer's reinterpretation of Christ. Bonhoeffer has replaced Christianity's element of the "religious" with the New Testament "man for others." It is, so to speak, another and different Jesus. An immediate question, therefore, is going to be: But what will become then of the doctrine of incarnation and divinity, especially as formulated by the great Christological councils? Robinson sees that this is what for many will block any attempt at reinterpretation. He goes ahead, nevertheless, and his approach at this spot is similar to van Buren's. First, he notes that modern biblical theology in general has already provided what van Buren considered an alternative. The New Testament, he argues, never simply says that Jesus was God, and the apologetic based upon Jesus' putative claim to be God takes a very wrong direction. For what Jesus claimed was that he brought God completely, and that in him God was working uniquely. Next, after supplying this bit of introduction from his own field of New Testament scholarship, Robinson takes up Bonhoeffer and "the man for others" theme directly.

He begins by stating that "all [Bonhoeffer] has left us is a single pregnant paragraph of notes for the 'outline for a book' he never lived to write: 'What do we mean by "God"? Not in the first place an abstract belief in his omnipotence, etc. That is not a genuine experience of God, but a partial extension of the world. Encounter with Jesus Christ, implying a complete orientation of human being in the experience of Jesus as one whose only concern is for others. This concern of Jesus for others the experience of transcendence. This freedom from self, maintained to the point of death, the sole ground of this omnipotence, omniscience and ubiquity. Faith in participation in this Being of Jesus (incarnation, cross and resurrection). Our relation to God not a religious relationship to a supreme Being, absolute in power and goodness, which is a spurious conception of transcendence, but a new life for others, through participation in the Being of God'." For Bonhoeffer, therefore, and now for Robinson, Christianity is not centered upon God, but upon Jesus, and upon Jesus conceived precisely as "the man for others." In the same sense, Christianity is "religionless."

Two things should be noted here. On the one hand, and this is what makes Robinson's appropriation of Bonhoeffer so much more positive than van Buren's, Robinson preserves intact Bonhoeffer's paradox. If God must give way to Jesus, if religion must henceforth be banished from Christianity, it is ultimately only God and religion as falsely conceived. For a bit earlier in the same fourth chapter, Robinson uses the same vehemence to attack *naturalism* that he uses to attack *supranaturalism*—and this is the passage in which he ends up siding, however begrudgingly, with Nicaea and Athanasius. But even more telling is another passage toward the very end of the book: "Nothing that has been said so far should be taken to imply that an indispensable task of the Church is not what the Collect calls the 'increase' of 'true religion.'. . . Unless the Church has the 'secret discipline' of which Bonhoeffer spoke as the presupposition of all his 'worldly Christianity,' unless the Christian's 'life is hid with Christ in God,' then any distinction between being *in* the world but not *of* it disappears, and at once he is down one side of the 'knife-edge'." Unmistakably, then, Bonhoeffer's Chris, tianity demands what is in the final analysis not only a theistic, but even a religious, context. So likewise does Robinson's. On the other hand, if Robinson thus remains perfectly faithful to Bonhoeffer, he does not really add anything of his own.

One is not surprised, therefore, to see the next pair of chapters, the fifth and sixth, offer Robinson's personal ideas on how Bonhoeffer's basic insight might be translated into Christian conduct in the two main areas of liturgics and ethics. First, he actually does develop a bit, at least pedagogically, the "religionless" concept as such. For instance, we can all recognize the difference, he tells us, between a film that is described as "religious" and a film that is described as "Christian." The latter simply embodies Christian insights, evaluations, situations, and without being the slightest bit "religious." The former, on the other hand, covers a particular area of experience, and is sometimes even nauseatingly unchristian. With the stage thus set, Robinson goes on to incorporate many excellent ideas from the modern liturgical revival, which is, of course, one of his own most vital concerns. The liturgy must not foster apartness, but rather be made to purify and instruct, that in this exercise the Christian might come to catch the depth ($=$ God . . . eventually) of the common, and learn to move through the world to God. Next, he turns to the field of contemporary Christian ethics, and makes much of the biblical scholar's observation that Christ did not give a new "law," but rather freedom from the law. In our judgment, however, Robinson simply raises the problem of the "intrinsically evil" and leaves it dangling. Also, since the points he introduces both now in the ethical and a moment earlier in the liturgical areas are shared by many others today, it is not quite clear that Robinson's development here is really a development of Bonhoeffer and Secularization. One is left with an impression of something missing, and with the feeling that to carry out Bonhoeffer, if that is his idea, what would be required would be a methodology altogether distinctive.

In any case, there is a seventh and final chapter. Will "Christianity" become as obsolete as "Christendom"? Robinson is not sure, but it might be inserted here that the echo of uncertainty left in *Honest to God* fades out in *The New Reformation?*: under the pressure of debate, no doubt, and the need to assess more closely the implications behind several of his hunches, Robinson's confidence in "Christianity," and even in the strictly institutional Church, will be more than a little restored. In the earlier book, however, he simply asks the question of ultimate survival, and turns to the meantime. He has no wish, he insists, to abandon Christianity, despite the likelihood that many will interpret his remarks to amount to that. But his purpose is really quite the opposite: to prevent, if possible, the necessity of abandoning Christianity. And the only way to do that is by recasting the mould.

So the controlling mood of *Honest to God* is pastoral and constructive, and it is charged throughout with Robinson's almost pathological optimism and buoyancy. Moreover, he would like to conclude by offering some specifics. Yet, this will not be easy. For "it is much harder to give a positive answer to [the] string of tantalizing questions posed by Bonhoeffer: 'What is the significance of a Church (church, parish, preaching, Christian life) in a religionless world? . . . In what way are we in a religionless and secular sense Christians, in what way are we the *Ekklesia,* "those who are called forth," not conceiving of ourselves religiously as specially favoured, but as wholly belonging to the world'?" Now to cite this particular passage from Bonhoeffer not at the beginning but at the end of the book could strike the reader as somewhat odd. Has not Robinson's entire study been precisely an attempt to answer Bonhoeffer's questions and implement his suggested program? But here we learn that it has not. By and large, his purpose has been the much more humble one of bringing Bonhoeffer's challenge to the English-speaking audience of the nineteen sixties. Robinson does not fancy himself as having added to that challenge in any serious way or degree.

Right at the very end, however, and while appealing to Yves Congar's concept of "laicity," the bishop does come close for a moment to a more than purely horizontal development of Bonhoeffer. In our surmise, there is at least a remote suggestion here of the kind of development undertaken by Cox: that is, of letting the secular forms not merely be accepted into Christianity, but express themselves and thereby actually instruct and reform Christianity. But this is only a surmise, and it may not be correct. In any case, Robinson rather quickly leaves the theme, and his book.

When compared with *Honest to God, The New Reformation?* serves a function of clarification, though it is our personal view that Robinson had not given anywhere near so much objective ground to the need for such clarification as his critics contended. Be that as it may, however, Robinson's profession of Christian faith is now made even more formal and explicit, and it is made to extend, as we have noted already, to the institutional Church precisely.

Also, there are some new features. Robinson now develops in greater detail—he had only adumbrated the theme in *Honest to God*—the symbolism of the "Servant Church." Undoubtedly, this has proved important for his restored confidence in the institutional Church: if it continues to be institutional, it is at the same time corrected in its very institutionalism, and remodeled on "the man for others." Another and quite delightful addition to Robinson's thought is his suggestion of the "good neighbor" apologetic as a more meaningful way of introducing the man of today's world to "the man for others." Finally, Robinson returns to the point of "laicity" with which he had concluded *Honest to God.* What Christianity needs at the moment is a "lay" theology. This would not be a theology "for the laity" (in the sense or senses to which we have grown accustomed), but a "theology which *starts* from the Christian's involvement in the world *now.*" It is not difficult to catch Robinson's general meaning here. The neat reversal—*from* the world *to* God, with the understanding that it is first *from* the world *to* Jesus as "the man for others"—communicates. On the other hand, it still seems, to the writer at least, that we could do with more detail, more specifics, the opening up of new and yet unexplored avenues of investigation that this fresh and positive approach to "wordliness" might be expected to suggest. But Robinson himself appears to be telling us, quite humbly, that he has not yet seen the light to define more precisely the lay and secularized theology which he nevertheless realizes we need. He quotes Bishop E. R. Wickham's remark that " 'it is surprising how little of the richness and variety of modern theological writing bites on the modern world'." And he obviously intends to include himself in what he adds in his own name immediately following: "Who, for instance, is producing a theology of power, of matter, of secularization and socialization, which are the real things which are shaping our lives? There seems to me an urgent need that a deliberate start should be made from the other end."

Let us turn next, then, to Harvey Cox and *The Secular City.* As we have already remarked, in a footnote in *The New Reformation?* Robinson mentions that he has actually read *The Secular City* in manuscript, but only after completing his own. Understandably, therefore, he was able to make only marginal use of precisely those analyses that might have given him the clue for which he seems to have been waiting.

Cox's highly compact and carefully written Introduction calls for something more than mere summation. For later on, the study will tend to thin out, and the development that is really essential to the key points made in the Introduction will get a

bit lost in a flurry of "becauses" and "therefores" which seem
to come a lot closer on occasion to being collateral hunch than
part of the argument. Yet, the Introduction (all the more significantly if it had been composed last) accurately anticipates the
controlling insight and central theme. Cox is going to advance
the Bonhoeffer program by at least one decisive step, and one
that cannot be traced back, as in Robinson's case, to Bonhoeffer
as either simple restatement or purely horizontal elaboration. He
is going to argue that the worldliness of the world, and worldliness precisely, is preaching the Gospel, did so yesterday, is doing
so better today, and will be doing so better still tomorrow; that
the message lies, again precisely, in the progressively secularizing forms of contemporary society, just those forms which many
religious people consider evil or occasions for evil, that most of
the rest consider to be at least morally indifferent, but which are
in fact, and once we break the code, good, spiritually creative,
in a corrected sense that Bonhoeffer would not disdain truly
"religious," Christian finally and Gospel. To put it more simply,
Cox's contribution will consist in a spiritual definition—a specifically Christian and Gospel definition—of the secularizing
forms of today's technopolis.

He begins by explaining the meaning of the two key words
which he wants to use to describe the ethos of our time: *secularization* and *urbanization*. The two are interrelated. The first,
secularization, designates a way of thinking, a world-view, and
names a change in our understanding of our life together,
brought about as the cosmopolitan confrontations of urban life
exposed the relativity of the myths and hitherto unquestioned
human traditions. Secularization, therefore, is the result of urbanization, the way of thinking the result of the way of living.
Such a law exists: forms of living affect forms of understanding,
and vice versa. Thus, "in our day the secular metropolis stands
as both the pattern of our life together and the symbol of our
view of the world." For us, today, the universe is the "city of

man," "a field of human exploration and endeavor from which the gods have fled. The world has become man's task and man's responsibility." Secularization is the name for the process by which all of this has come to be. And urbanization, the second key word, simply designates the new style of life, itself the product ultimately of science and technology, which generates the new world-view.

Secularization, to carry the descriptive analysis further, is what C. A. van Peursen thinks of as "the deliverance of man 'first from religious and then from metaphysical control over his reason and his language'." Next, Cox introduces Bonhoeffer: "It is what Dietrich Bonhoeffer in 1944 called 'man's coming of age'." But this, in Cox' mind, merely represented the theologian's tardy effort to interpret what poets, novelists, sociologists and philosophers had been observing for decades.

We must not envision secularization, on the other hand, as anticlerical, antireligious, or anti-Christian. For "it has relativized religious world-views and thus rendered them innocuous." Under its influence, religion has simply been "privatized" into being henceforth the concern only of the individual or the particular group.

At this point, Cox calls a momentary halt. Has secularization really succeeded in toppling the gods? What of such patently religious events and movements as the self-immolation of Buddhist monks, the whole Black Muslim affair in the United States, the signs of new vigor throughout Roman Catholicism? But Cox retorts the objection neatly: the seeming exceptions are born of a secular context and a secular spirit. It is nationalism that really inspires the revival of the Oriental religions, and a strictly secularist pluralism that motivates the Roman Catholic reassessment and displaces what had been yesterday's closed system. When all is said and done, "the age of the secular city, the epoch whose ethos is quickly spreading into every corner of the globe, *is* an age of 'no religion at all'." And Cox goes on to tick off how today's world has become, in the Bonhoeffer sense, "religion-less." It no longer takes religion as the supplier of moral rules, but only as a hobby perhaps, or a mark of group identification, or simply a matter of esthetic delight. Even Communism is rapidly losing its "religious" quality.

Cox now concludes, in a very important single paragraph, his initial description of secularization: "Secularization rolls on, and if we are to understand and communicate with our present age we must learn to love it *in its unremitting secularity* [emphasis added]. We must learn, as Bonhoeffer said, to speak of God in a secular fashion and find a non-religious interpretation of biblical concepts." Up to this moment, and apart from the broadly sociological structure of his analysis, Cox has added little or nothing to the theology of a Secularization movement as conceived by Bonhoeffer and then by Robinson. But it is here that he goes off on his own. There is a hint in his reference to having to love the world "in its unremitting secularity." Then he adds a moment later: "[Religious and metaphysical versions of Christianity] are disappearing forever and that means we can now let go and immerse ourselves in the new world of the secular city. The first step in such an immersion is learning something about its peculiar characteristics." This is the key to what Cox is saying in *The Secular City*. The language is straight-forward and unimpressive: we must begin by learning the secular city's "peculiar characteristics." But what Cox means by these "peculiar characteristics" is the unsuspectingly spiritual and Christian characteristics of the non-religious certainly, very much ordinary and taken-for-granted forms of our secularized society—to take two examples he will develop later, the un-suspectingly spiritual and Christian characteristics of present-day "mobility" and "anonymity." For the moment, this is all Cox will say. Having completed his description of the first key word, "secularization," he has now to describe in parallel fashion the second key word, "urbanization."

"If secularization," he starts off, "designates the content of man's coming of age, urbanization describes the context in which it is occurring. It is the 'shape' of the new society which supports its peculiar style." Social scientists, to be sure, may differ on just what urbanization ought to mean, but they will agree that it is at least not merely a quantitative notion (population size, etc.). Nor is urbanization limited to the city proper, for such urban phenomena as high mobility, economic concentration and mass communications extend to the rural village.

More positively, "urbanization means a structure of common life in which diversity and the disintegration of tradition are paramount. It means a type of impersonality in which functional relationships multiply. It means that a degree of tolerance and anonymity replace traditional moral sanctions and long-term acquaintanceships. The urban center is the place of human control, of rational planning, of bureaucratic organization—and the urban center is not just in Washington, London, New York, and Peking. It is everywhere. The technological metropolis provides the indispensable social setting for a world of 'no religion at all', for what we have called a secular style."

To describe urbanization, therefore, Cox talks about the "shape" of our society, a word which is going to make us think more of material and physical than moral or spiritual things; and also about setting and context, words which will suggest to us an element of remoteness, background, predisposition perhaps, or occasion, or opportunity. To describe secularization, he talks rather about the style, and the content. The two classifications, however, must not be divided too sharply. Pragmatism, as an attitude, belongs to the style and the content, and comes closer to the moral and theological order, obviously, than does mobility, which belongs to the shape. But in Cox's mind, there attaches even to mobility, though more remotely, a strictly moral and theological value. And we could note, of course, the examples of more clearly moral and theological forms in the passage on urbanization just quoted. There, Cox included diversity, an element of cultural shape that puts us on the same level as mobility so far as distance from the explicitly moral and theological is concerned. But he also included tolerance, and although from the context it was a predispositive and more or less sub-ethical tolerance that he probably was thinking about, a tolerance scarcely distinguishable from the phenomena of pluralism, nonetheless the distance from the explicitly moral and theological in this second example narrows significantly.

The most important section of Part One, following the Introduction, and perhaps the most important section of the entire book, will be devoted to a further examination into this closely interlocked shape and style of the secular city.

As the Introduction itself continues, Cox turns next to the categories of cultural history to discuss secularization as an epoch. Three distinct epochs, in fact, are pinpointed: that of the tribe, that of the town, and that of the modern technopolis—the third and last being given the name "technopolis" simply to designate the urbanized community with specific attention to "the fusion of technological and political components into the base on which a new cultural style has appeared." The three epochs, to be sure, are neither merely successive nor discontinuous; not only does continuity exist, but also residue: one can find a tribal mentality in residents of New York City. All in all, however, it remains that the "technopolitan culture is the wave of the future."

Cox begins, then, with the tribe, the already social setting in which man becomes man. However tribal society be defined, and for all the need there may be to recognize personal differences within the general class, experts agree on one extremely important point: this is the correlation between a given economic level of society and the kind of supernatural beings postulated by the group or individuals within. As Cox puts it succinctly, "when man changes his tools and his techniques, his ways of producing and distributing the goods of life, he also changes his gods." Hence, tribal society does exhibit certain common features which we can analyze. Basically, the tribe is an expanded family, compact and enclosed, with tradition dictating the form of all relationships. It cannot withstand prolonged contact with the outside. But this is exactly what happens. And so the tribe becomes the town. In the process, "man moves from a belief in ghosts and demons to a belief in gods, from spells and incantations to prayers, from shamans and sorcerers to priests and teachers, from myth and magic to religion and theology." But "all of this happens only when the economic structure of the society allows for a group of self-conscious religious specialists to emerge."

Tribal society left each individual secure in an assigned identity and role; it solved the basic problems of marriage and occupation without raising them. On the other hand, tribal man was "hardly a personal 'self' in our modern sense of the word." He was little more than "the tribe's subjective expression." The transition, therefore, from tribal society to town society was one of history's decisive breakthroughs. In a word, tribal man had to be liberated, and it is all-important to see how the liberation became concretely possible.

It is "the appearance of currency and the development of the alphabet [that] supply two essential ingredients in the shattering step from tribe to town." Cox adds immediately the reason why: "Both devices tend to free individuals from traditionally prescribed relationships and to expand enormously the possible occasions for human contact." But it is essential to the message of *The Secular City* that we grasp, from the over-all context and later development of the study, everything that is implied in this reason as Cox understands it. The two devices which he mentions, currency and alphabet, liberate the individual from the extraordinary restrictions that characterized tribal life in the areas of transaction and communication. Currency and alphabet, therefore, make the town a possibility. For they produce that freedom from traditionally prescribed relationships and that expansion of occasions for human contact upon which town society is based. But the freedom and expansion here might seem to be hardly more than mechanical. Cox's ultimate point, however, is that the same devices which make possible the town, and in the very same cultural process, make possible a more mature and strictly moral human decision and responsibility. The now vastly broadened opportunities for transaction and communication make possible, foster and encourage the greater exercise of decision and responsibility. And in Cox's mind this is precisely what happens again at the second and later transition, this time from the town to the technopolis. The "essential ingredients" in this next and equally shattering step are all the devices of scientific technology that produce modern urbanization with the new freedom and the new expansion of occasions for human contact that exist in our modern transportation, our modern bureaucratic structure and our modern functional relationship.

Such, then, for Cox is the movement, the forward movement, of cultural history. But it is also the movement of the Judaeo-Christian revelation. The key lies in the notion of human freedom and human responsibility. As the tribe became the town, the socio-economic new forms of that primitive stage of secularization encouraged precisely the same exercise of human freedom and the same assumption of human responsibility that is the authentic message of the Christian Gospel.

When tribal man had to barter, for instance, what he would give and what he would take in return, the personalities and circumstances of the exchange, were all rather rigidly controlled, and therefore so was his own life and his family. But once he could sell what he had and with the money pick what he would buy, he was rendered at once more mobile and more independent. Similarly, as writing developed, tribal man's original access to information became depersonalized, and this too made him that much more independent. Formerly, he had had to rely totally on the person of the shaman or the oracle. From now on, he could begin to learn for himself. And as this freedom and independence grew, so also did the opportunities for decision and responsibility.

The discussion about writing brings Cox to comment on an important difference between the tribe and the town, and the comment in turn leads to a direct consideration of the New Testament. In the tribe, there could be no admission of strangers. In the town, however, and despite difficulties, the greatly extended base for human contact made it possible for strangers and outsiders to become citizens. But "this transformation of 'strangers and outsiders' into 'fellow citizens and members one of another' recalls, of course, an expression close to the heart of the New Testament message (see Ephesians 2). It suggests one good reason why the early church, from its outset a detribalizing movement in which there was 'no longer Jew nor Greek', spread most quickly in the towns and cities."

In this respect, Cox continues, the early Church was far ahead of the polis. Athens, Rome too, each with its fictional common ancestor, and with a slavery and imperialism irreconcilable with universal citizenship, remained in part a tribe. Thus, two reasons can be given why Athens never became a modern metropolis. The first and obvious one is that modern scientific technology had not yet set the stage. "But the second is that the universality and radical openness of the Gospel was not yet present to dispel the remnants of tribalism. . . . Only after the beginning of the Christian era was the *idea* of an inclusive metropolis conceivable, and even then it took nearly two millennia to realize it."

Cox's idea here is not that an element of Christian teaching influenced the progress of urbanization *de facto,* but rather that the very heart of the Christian message—universal charity— made the transition from the town to the technopolis radically possible. The same theme, the strictly formative role of the

Judaeo-Christian revelation in the secularization of culture, is expanded in the very next section, the first chapter of Part One.

Part One is entitled "The Coming of the Secular City." Cox discusses first its biblical origin, secondly its shape and style.

What had been anticipated in the Introduction, and what will occupy Cox now in his first chapter is neatly summarized at the beginning: "Secularization, as the German theologian Friedrich Gogarten once remarked, is the legitimate consequence of the impact of biblical faith on history. This is why it is no mere accident that secularization arose first within the culture of the so-called Christian West, in the history within which the biblical religions have made their most telling impact. The rise of natural science, of democratic political institutions, and of cultural pluralism—all developments we normally associate with Western culture—can scarcely be understood without the original impetus of the Bible. Even though the conscious connection has long since been lost sight of, the relationships are still there." To elaborate, Cox proposes to show "how three pivotal elements in the biblical faith have each given rise to one aspect of secularization."

Presecular tribal man lived in a world alive with enchantment, the enchantment of what man calls today nature. Even the Sumerian, Egyptian and Babylonian societies preserved the basically magical world-view, but in a more sophisticated form. In fact, and as many historians of religion agree, it was only as the biblical idea of creation separated nature from God and man from nature that sun, moon, stars, all the things of nature, lost their divinity and became, in Max Weber's word, "disenchanted." But this disenchantment was the absolutely essential precondition for the development of natural science, and hence of eventual urbanization.

Again, in the world of presecular man whoever ruled ruled by divine right and with divine identification. But with the biblical Exodus, that "massive act of what we might today call 'civil disobedience'," and which "became the central event around which the Hebrews organized their whole perception of reality," politics, as previously nature, was likewise separated from God. And in this "desacralization" of politics, lie the roots of the possibility of political and social transformation.

Finally, if neither nature nor politics are any longer simply extensions and expressions of divinity, neither is modern man's whole pattern of values. For everything has become relativized. But what ultimately effected this radical "deconsecration" of values was the Sinai Covenant, and more particularly its prohibition, revolutionary at the time, of the worship of human idols. And to this ancient biblical emancipation, is owed the farreaching pluralistic dimension of secularized society.

Cox is not arguing in this chapter that the liberation theme of the Old Testament revelation influenced society as a whole and in the pre-Christian period. He is arguing, rather, that the Judaeo-Christian revelation was itself frankly and deliberately "secularizationist" from its remote beginnings. By way of comment, we would want to say that the creationist view of nature certainly disenchants nature; but so do, and did, other forces. Clearly, there is the element of political desacralization in the Exodus event and motif; but much the same element is found elsewhere. Finally, there is in fact a magnificent power for the image-breaking of falsely absolutized human values implicit in the Sinaitic Covenant and its great prohibition; but to want to associate this power exclusively and genetically with the Old Testament tradition, even while admitting that its historical impact would be much later on in the Christian era, at least seems to disregard the fact that ancient philosophies and sciences were producing, quite independently, parallel attitudes.

What *is* clear, on the other hand, is that the Judaeo-Christian revelation, as it came to term in the New Testament, and as the more primitive "disenchantments," "desacralizations," "deconsecrations," emerged totally transformed in a higher simplicity, impels to personal freedom and socio-cultural responsibility. Perhaps Cox should have been content to emphasize this?

The Old Testament flash-back has the value of showing that the Christian message, not only in its definitive stage, but from its remote beginnings in the Hebrew past, was moving in the same direction as cultural evolution. The further question as to whether the biblical message actually has guided cultural evolution does not arise in any serious way until the Christian period, and even then must be handled carefully: some, even vast, guidance of a direct sort would be almost impossible to deny; but exclusive guidance, even in what respects the maturation of personal freedom and socio-cultural responsibility, equally impossible to defend. To our mind, however, this is not the significant issue. The significant issue is the ultimate sameness of direction. The Bible moves with the world and the world with the Bible—the world precisely in its worldliness, moreover, which is not, of course, the world in its aberrations and its mistakes, but the world in the evolving socio-economic patterns that directly enlarge the scope of freedom and responsibility.

Cox gets back to these patterns in the two chapters immediately following. These are the chapters on the "shape" and "style" respectively of the secular city. Because of their importance, in the final pages of our own first chapter we had already given them some detailed consideration. What will concern us now, therefore, will be their function in extending the argument based upon freedom and responsibility more precisely.

When discussing in his Introduction the transition from tribal society to town society, Cox drew attention to the liberating role of currency and alphabet. Now he wishes to point out the repetition and intensification of the same liberating—spiritually liberating—process in the anonymity and mobility of the urbanized metropolis.

Taking first anonymity, Cox notes the long and impressive list of philosophers, poets and novelists who in our day have flayed against this particular characteristic of modern living. But in Cox's judgment, "a writer who becomes *essentially* anti-urban forfeits his claim to greatness, for what is often left unsaid by the morbid critics of anonymity is, first, that without it, life in a modern city could not be human, and second, that anonymity represents for many people a liberating even more than a threatening phenomenon. It serves for large numbers of people as the possibility of freedom in contrast to the bondage of the law and convention." It is this "possibility of freedom," especially as understood in a Christian and Gospel context, that Cox wishes to emphasize.

Urbanized man is free to choose from an immensely widened range of possibilities—extending all the way from the choice of one out of fifty different movies to the choice, at least in some measure, of a job or prospective marriage partner. But the freedom demands a certain discipline. What is not chosen, what is excluded, is consciously excluded. With so many more "contacts" within his reach, urban man has to limit himself and pick wisely his circle of intimates. The unlisted phone expresses this necessity. Its purpose is not cold, heartless and depersonalizing, but quite the opposite. It is the user's way of protecting his personal privacy, and with that privacy his more intimate personal relationships. For urban man must be particularly careful to observe the distinction between the personal and the functional relationship. This is not, however, so that he will treat some people as "things," the idea so abhorrent to the existentialists, but simply so that he will treat them as not in every way his intimates.

Theologically, the key to the interpretation of the profound anonymity of urbanized society, Cox continues, is, once more, liberation, liberation from the past and from the bondage of human convention. He understands this, moreover, not as liberation in general, but as the liberation chartered in the Judaeo-Christian revelation in terms of the passing from Law to Gospel.

"[Law] is what Riesman calls the power of 'other-direction' driving us toward conformity to the expectations and customs of the culture, enforced in a thousand small, nearly unnoticeable ways by the people who make our choices for us. When Law rather than Gospel becomes the basis for our lives, it militates against choice and freedom. It decides for us, thus sapping our powers of responsibility. Similarly, Gospel in a broader sense means a summons to choice and answerability." And Cox returns immediately to the deeper theme of the sameness of direction as observed between the movement of cultural history and the movement of the biblical message: "Our use of the Law-Gospel dialectic here suggests that it has a broader relevance than is ordinarily accorded it in theology. It suggests that in the historical process itself man meets the One who calls him into being as a free deciding self, and knows that neither his past history nor his environment determines what he does."

On the practical side, Cox notes that "often a nagging sense of guilt plagues the urban man with rural roots because he cannot possibly cultivate an I-Thou relationship with everyone. Unfortunately the church, largely bound to a preurban ethos, often exacerbates his difficulty by seeking to promote small-town intimacy among urban people and by preaching the necessity of I-Thou relationships as the only ones that are really human. But this represents a misreading of the Gospel and a disservice to urban man. Relationships among urbanites do not have to be lifeless or heartless just because they are impersonal. . . . We need to develop a viable theology of anonymity. In doing so, it might be useful to add another type of human relationship to Buber's famous pair. Besides 'I-It' relationships, in which the other person is reduced to the status of an object, and in addition to the profound, personally formative 'I-Thou' encounter, why could we not evolve a theology of the 'I-You' relationship? Buber's philosophy suffers from an unnecessary dichotomy."

Cox turns next to mobility. Modern urban man is constantly on the go, to work, to play, to everything. The same aura of movement, the same speed of getting things done, has invaded the rural world beyond the inner city. This mobility, moreover, no less than anonymity, has provided a favorite target for the philosophers, poets and novelists who see in it the cause of present-day man's rootlessness and the doom of a homeless wanderer. (Significantly, however, American writers have long recognized that mobility had at least a brighter side.)

As Cox notes, it is residential and occupational mobility in particular that comes in for the harshest criticism. Yet, he considers much of the celebration of the homestead and the life-time job little more than the pseudo-religious romanticism of the fundamentally reactionary mind. Worse still, since such residential and occupational mobility is exactly an essential factor in social change and the emancipation of the hitherto underprivileged, the enthusiasm for its opposite is often just another ruse of class oppression.

In any case, there can be no serious question about the fact that without today's extraordinary mobility in such key areas as communication, transportation, the pursuit of a career, the urban metropolis would, as Cox observes, strangle. But this is on a quite material level, it might be objected. There remains very much a question about the effect of the same mobility on religion.

Cox admits candidly that mobility is disruptive of religion, of a type of religion certainly, and at least at one level: it separates the individual from his sanctuary while at the same time admitting into the sanctuary what is alien. But mobility also has a strictly positive side as a vital element in urbanization. Cox feels that there is no need to argue the general point any further than he has already apropos of his discussion of anonymity. He believes that he has sufficiently demonstrated the spiritual character, though he does not call it that, of urbanization; what is essential to urbanization, even in a merely material sense, therefore, is spiritually creative.

However, Cox wants to show something else as well: the Judaeo-Christian revelation has always been linked to a context of mobility, and has always preserved an element of mobility both in its understanding of itself as a religion and in its very concept of its God. The primitive religious growth of Israel was in a nomadic and even disruptive setting, with periods of relative stability actually proving to be the less creative. "In short, when they were wandering and homeless the Jews seem to have been closest to fulfilling their calling." Yahweh himself was viewed as Lord of history and time, rather than of something sedentary or fixed; and "although the view of Yahweh as a nomadic, non-spatial God was constantly threatened by syncretism with the Canaanite Baal, it finally withstood the test." Cox goes on to develop the contrast between Yahweh and the Baalim in this regard. Next, he points to the further and parallel contrast between Israel's Ark of the Covenant and the Inca temple, or the Egyptian sphinx, or the Babylonian ziggurat. And, more significantly still, Yahweh was free from the confines of the Ark when it was captured. As Cox concludes, "This whole historical movement by which Yahweh was divested of spatiality has enormous theological significance. It meant that Yahweh could not be localized at any given geographic spot. He traveled with his people and elsewhere."

The nomadic culture of the Hebrews, then, inspired a highly mobile God-view. And in the New Testament, Jesus continued this tradition of opposition to "sacred places and holy homelands." Cox appeals, for example, to his rejection in the Transfiguration story of the permanent monument, but most of all to his identification of the new temple with his own risen body. Thus, from earliest times, authentic Christianity has always preserved its sense of mobility, homelessness, pilgrimage. On the other hand, it has only been as Christianity in its concrete form became respatialized in later centuries to appear as the "religion of Western Europe" that "Christianity" passed into "Christendom"—and this was a betrayal, a betrayal that is in process of being reversed today.

Cox ends his treatment of modern mobility on a modest note of pro and con: "Mobility is not the menace religious romantics paint it. It has its pitfalls. Endless movement from place to place can betray the same kind of unwillingness to take responsibility for decisions which can be seen in switching wives. But by and large the mobile man is less tempted than the immobile man to demote Yahweh into a baal. He will usually not idolatrize any town or nation. He will not be as likely to see the present economic and political structure as the unambiguous expression of how things always have been and always should be. He will be more open to change, movement, newness. There is no reason why Christians should deplore the accelerating mobility of the modern metropolis. The Bible does not call man to renounce mobility, but to 'go to a place that I will show unto you'. . . . High mobility is no assurance of salvation, but neither is it an obstacle to faith."

At the beginning of his study, Cox had proposed to describe both the "shape" and the "style" of the secular city. The "shape" is the context—urbanization—and Cox has just broken it down for us into the two components of anonymity and mobility. The "style" is the content—secularization—and Cox will now break this down also, into the key attitudes of pragmatism and profanity that are fundamental to the secularized world-view. The further analysis of urbanization, with the isolation of anonymity and mobility, helped to clarify what exactly in the urban setting fostered the exercise of freedom and the assumption of responsibility—what it was, therefore, that made the world move in the same direction as the Gospel. Similarly, the further analysis of secularization, with the isolation of pragmatism and profanity, will help clarify how the secular mind articulates its very secularity at the moment of living the life of such freedom and responsibility.

One must be careful, moreover, not to conceive the relationship between the urbanized "shape" and the secularized "style" solely in terms of the former's influence upon the latter. For the influence here is quite reciprocal: "The secular-urban style springs in part from the societal shape provided by the anonymity and mobility we have just discussed. But it is not merely a product of these factors. The style has a life of its own which in turn influences and alters the shape on which it is based."

The pragmatic man, in Cox's sense, is the man who is preoccupied with whether or not a thing will work, with results, with what lies within the scope of the here and now possible, rather than with ultimates. This, of course, is precisely the network of preoccupations which the traditionalist insists modern man must lay aside if he is to hear the message of the Gospel. But Cox believes that Bonhoeffer has silenced the objection once and for all.

We have seen how, as exemplifying the ideal of today's pragmatic man, the man the dictionary describes as concerned with "practical or material affairs" and interested in the "actual working out of an idea in experience," Cox cites John F. Kennedy. But it is the pragmatic discipline that he wishes most to stress. For if the pragmatic man does not operate from a minutely conceptualized ideological system, he nevertheless does operate systematically. He sees existence as a series of problems demanding workable solutions. He must know what the problem is, and be able to separate it from the irrelevant; he must determine what is within the concrete reach of accomplishment and what is not; then he must act decisively for the here and now, and with every expectation that the immediate solution will quite naturally give rise to a whole new set of problems. Throughout this entire process, moreover, he must often be assisted by the teams of experts that constitute such a typical aspect of contemporary bureaucratic society.

As in the sections preceding when dealing with anonymity and mobility, Cox turns explicitly to the Judaeo-Christian revelation in order to examine from this all-important viewpoint the pragmatic style thus outlined. Following van Peursen once again, Cox envisions modern man as having passed from the "ontological" to the "functional" period of human history, from the view of reality in terms of "substances" to the view of reality in terms of "what to do." Does this contradict the biblical tradition? Neither van Peursen nor Cox thinks so.

The crux of the argument lies in the interpretation of the Hebrew word for truth (*'emeth*) as actually meaning what can be counted on. However, the argument, as Cox has left it, is somewhat unsatisfactory. It tries to prove too much, and what it does prove seems to add little to what has been said already. That the Old Testament "truth" vocabulary would often more accurately be rendered by words suited to express directly the fidelity and reliance associated with the Covenant relationship, is a valid observation, and of course not a new one. Likewise, it is obvious that the Old Testament notions of "truth" were not in Cox's sense "ontological." When the argument, then, is used to show that the Old Testament, and subsequently the New, encourage a dedication to the immediate and the practical—in the context of what one can here and now rely upon—it has a degree of merit. When it is simultaneously used, as seems to be Cox's intention, to diminish the value of more sophisticated notions of truth that emerged later, it is logically ineffective and succeeds only in distracting from the real task at hand. For Cox's ultimate purpose here is simply to show, once again, the biblical orientation toward the exercise of personal freedom and the assumption of socio-cultural responsibility, as comes out quite clearly at the end of the passage.

And it comes out more clearly still in the section immediately

following where Cox discusses the second basic attitude compos-
ing the "style" of secularization, profanity. He does not mean,
of course, vulgarity; and perhaps in light of the almost inescap-
able contrary suggestion "profaneness" would communicate the
idea more securely. For the perspective or world-view thus named
is nothing else than Bonhoeffer's "secular manner" and Robinson's "this-worldliness" in a slightly more specific guise. To il-
lustrate, Cox introduces the personality, and something of the
expressed personal philosophy, of Albert Camus. The example,
however, may not be the best, nor the most consistent with
Cox's theme: throughout he has been at great pains to distinguish carefully between "secularization" and "secularism," but
secularization as instanced in Camus seems to be more doctrinaire than merely stylistic, and this is not what Cox wants.

In any case, Camus "insisted that man must choose between
the tyrant God of Christian theology and being a full man.
Having made this choice, man could then turn his full attention
to striving for justice 'as often as the opportunity is given'. I believe that the choice Camus presents us with is an unavoidable
one, and that given the choice as he understood it, we can only
choose with him. A god who emasculates man's creativity and
hamstrings his responsibility for his fellow man must be de-
throned. Nietzsche and Marx as well as Proudhon saw this. The
difference is that in our period the issue is being forced not by
a few scattered intellectuals who style themselves atheists, but
by the whole character of urban-secular civilization." The key
point being made here, and the heart of Cox's entire thesis, is
seen in the words "a God who emasculates man's creativity and
hamstrings his responsibility for his fellow man." *This* is the
"God" that has to go, this "God" and this type of "religion"—
ultimately, therefore, and as earlier with Bonhoeffer, God and
religion as falsely conceived. In this same gloss on Camus, Cox
gives us as well the more positive reason why: it is because any
true religion, any true following of the true God, must neces-

sarily emphasize precisely, and just as secularization does, "man's creativity" and "his responsibility for his fellow man." This, moreover, is precisely the challenge of the Judaeo-Christian revelation.

For Camus, it has to be either God or human responsibility, and so Camus chooses to be atheist. For Cox, however, this is to ignore or at least misread the biblical message, and he makes one final, rather telling, appeal to the text of the Old Testament. Right in Genesis, in the very narrative in which creation of the world by God is the matter of emphasis and elaboration, human creativity and responsibility is likewise emphasized and elaborated. In the "naming of the animals," man's subordinate, but entirely real, role *in creation* is carefully described. Cox's argument here, borrowing heavily from von Rad, is worth quoting at some length: "For the Hebrew, naming did not mean simply attaching an arbitrary label. It meant conferring on something its meaning and significance. As Gerhard von Rad says, the naming of the animals is the way man 'incorporates them into his life'. The act of naming here is an original and creative one. Man does not 'form' the animals, but he does give them their names. Yet naming and forming must not be too widely separated. As God begins his activity in Genesis 1, the earth is described as 'without form' and 'void'. God's creative activity includes forming, separating, and naming. Then, after He creates man, He enlists him in this creating activity. Thus the world does not come to man already finished and ordered. It comes in part confused and formless and receives its significance from man. Since man names the animals, the meaning they have comes from the fact that they are incorporated into his life. Their significance arises from their being a part of his projects and purposes. Von Rad goes on to remind us that 'name-giving in the ancient Orient was primarily an exercise of sovereignty, of command'. For this reason he holds that the animal-naming passage must be read in close connection with Genesis 1:28, where man is commanded by God to 'have dominion over the fish of the sea and over the birds of the air. . . .' Here is a truly exalted view of man. God does not simply insert man into a world filled with creatures which are already named, in relationships and meaning patterns already established by decree. Man must fashion them himself. He doesn't simply discover meaning; he originates it."

Now, it could perhaps be objected that what constitutes human creativity and human responsibility at the present moment of human evolution is so vastly more sophisticated than any remotely similar idea which might have been entertained by the ancient Hebrew writer, that Cox's quite direct comparison and application should be very much more critically nuanced. The writer has already stated, however, that he believes Cox's main insight to lie in the radical sameness of direction as observed both in the evolution of cultural history—hence in secularization—on the one side, and the Judaeo-Christian revelation, on the other. Further, he considers that the second element of the observation, the direction of the Judaeo-Christian revelation, can be established only by appeal to the biblical tradition as a whole, with the New Testament contribution in the final analysis absolutely essential.

But it is time to note that even this latter could be challenged. Does not the New Testament in fact make the very center of its message human freedom, human creativity, human responsibility, and do so with the utter clarity Cox's thesis demands? Is not the central message of the New Testament in fact universal charity?

The truth of the matter, however, is that we have to say yes, not to either one of these questions, but to both of them at once. Cox had at least implicitly identified the Christian stress on freedom and responsibility with the Christian stress on universal charity when he was in the process of arguing that only the latter made the definitive transition from tribe to town radically possible—with the understanding that by town one meant the real town as opposed to the pre-Christian town that retained so much of the tribe. Much more significantly, on the other hand, the ideal of freedom and responsibility underscored throughout the entire book is the freedom and responsibility of "the man for others." It is the exercise of personal freedom and the assumption of social and historical responsibility in total dedication to others, to humanity, precisely. And it is this because it was this for Jesus of Nazareth, "the Suffering Servant" and "the man for others." In the teaching of the New Testament, the career of "the Suffering Servant" who is "the man for others" *defines* the charity, the love, of Jesus; and the charity, the love of Jesus so defined is the unique example for all his followers.

In the present day, moreover, when so much is done or omitted on the facile appeal to charity and love, it may be useful to point out the fact that the very latest movement in contemporary theology wants to emphasize that the authentically biblical ideal of charity and love is inseparable from, even defined by, the mature exercise of personal freedom and the self-expending assumption of social and historical responsibility in dedication to humanity. Minus this definition, "Christ-like charity" may well wear the name, but hardly the reality.

At this juncture, it is tempting to continue on into the further Parts and chapters of *The Secular City,* but the temptation must be resisted. Our purpose is confrontation with the gradually emerging central issues rather than discussion of detail, particularly of such detail that represents further exemplification and application of the already recorded key insights. We shall have to limit ourselves, therefore, to the following quite general comments.

Cox has completed his main description of the ultimately Christian shape and style of the secular city. Two questions, therefore, immediately come into mind. First, what should be the bearing of all this upon our idea of the nature and role of the Church? Secondly, how should it affect our concept of God?

From a larger point of view, of course, both of these questions had been present from the beginning. If the course of secularization, and in this sense "of the world," has taken the same overall direction as that indicated by the Judaeo-Christian revelation, the Church, insofar as it defines itself in relation to the world, is already being conceived in a somewhat new light. And a somewhat new attitude, obviously, is being recommended to govern its activity. Right from the Introduction, moreover, it is clear that at least a particular concept of God is being systematically excluded. But Cox will now try to get down to cases.

He begins with the Church, or more precisely with the context in which the question of the Church must be approached. "The starting point for any theology of the church today must be a theology of social change." For this, there is needed a meaningful symbol, something to assist contemporary ecclesiology in breaking away from the "ideology of preservation and permanence" and orientation to a past. Cox suggests the symbol of "the secular city." The value of this symbol lies in the fact that it serves to emphasize technopolis as "an emergent reality" specifically, and hence to put parallel emphasis on the ideals of "maturation and responsibility." To continue his argument, Cox must first dismiss the classical objections: that the secular city is the work of man; that the Gospel demands its renunciation; that the Kingdom of God, on the other hand, is beyond and above history. But to handle these objections, he has only to add to the sameness of direction principle the contemporary theology of a realized eschatology. Secondly, he must show the special aptitude of the secular city symbol in the service of bonafide revolutionary theory. And this he does by pointing to the power of secularization to catalyze action, to interpret the hitherto inaction, to purge from this inaction, and finally to introduce an understanding of catastrophe and the social dénouement. Hence it is, in Cox's mind, that "the idea of the secular city supplies us with the most promising image by which *both* to understand what the New Testament writers called 'the Kingdom of God' *and* to develop a viable theology of revolutionary social change."

In such a context, and only in such a context, is Cox prepared to discuss qualitatively the nature and role of the Church. On the negative side, he wishes to stress the point that "the church is not in the first instance an institution." For, as he goes on immediately, the biblical revelation itself thinks of it primarily as the "people of God." Cox, of course, is not alone in making this initial point; it had been made, in fact, by so traditionally oriented a document as the Constitution *Lumen Gentium* of Vatican II. And if Cox's further statements on the nature of the Church in *The Secular City* seem, as certain of his critics thought, to reduce the institutional element to the vanishing point, he is at pains to correct this impression in the subsequently published Afterword that concludes *The Secular City Debate.*

Positively, however, his chief concern is to describe the triple function of the Church—kerygmatic, diakonic, koinoniac—in terms of a secularized, but still therefore authentically biblical, theology. As kerygmatic, the Church is not uttering propositions, but issuing a summons; the summons is to freedom from every manner of constraining force, and to the assumption of personal and social responsibility. As diakonic, the Church is engaged, yes, in service; but service, for Cox, is too weak a word; the true diakonic responsibility is rather that of healing and reconciling the profound ills and fractures of urbanized existence. As koinoniac, the Church achieves the "visible demonstration of what [it] is saying in its kerygma and pointing to in its diakonia."

The seventh chapter, entitled "The Church as Cultural Exorcist," completes the analysis of the nature and role of the Church that takes up Part Two, and paves the way for the "Excursions in Urban Exorcism" of Part Three. That Cox would make so much of this theme, is exactly what we should expect. It is the reverse side of the coin of which the ideal of freedom and responsibility is the other. For there can be no freedom and responsibility so long as individuals and society remain "possessed" by the forces of immature and unhealthy psychology. This, he adds, is precisely what lies behind the "prescientific images" which we encounter in the Gospel accounts of Jesus' own exorcisms. "In the New Testament, Jesus' confrontation with the demons represents his battle against projected fantasies, and his attack on the Scribes and Pharisees who were the custodians of ritual meticulousness dramatizes his struggle against compulsive behavior patterns." Cox sums up what this means, and has to mean, for the Church today: "The ministry of the church in the secular city does include a contemporary extension of exorcism. Men must be called away from their fascination with other worlds—astrological, metaphysical, or religious—and summoned to confront the concrete issues of this one, 'wherein alone the true call of God can be found'. They must be freed from the narcotic vagaries through which they wrongly perceive the social reality around them, and from habitual forms of action or inaction stemming from these illusions. This is the work of social exorcism. It was carried out by Jesus; his church should be expected to carry on this same work."

Application is first made to the field of work. In Part One, Cox had attempted to demonstrate that the anonymity and mobility which characterize the shape of today's urban metropolis are not forces of dissolution and evil—not automatically certainly—but forces of great potential spiritual and Christian good. Now he merely extends that observational insight a bit further. Just as there have been a lot of wasted tears over man the faceless cipher and rootless wanderer, so have there been a lot more over the "functionalization" and "defamilialization" of work that follows upon the separation of work and residence. Rhapsodizing about the dear old "family farm" is worse than useless; it is gone, and we do not want to bring it back. For at bottom, the separation of work and residence is simply another human and social emancipation. In the same vein, there is like-

wise little merit in bemoaning the sad fate of today's "organization man." For the bureaucratic "organization" is here to stay,
and when we examine it more closely we cannot help but
observe its flexibility, its orientation to the future, its healthy
secularization, and the ultimate limitation of its much-heralded
power over its members. What the organization really means is
a profound "dereligionization" of work, and a consequent increase in the opportunities for free decision and responsible
commitment. As Cox concludes, "secularization liberates man for
work by emptying work of the almost neurotic compulsiveness
and the religious mystery in which it has been enshrouded in
Western society since the monastic period and the Reformation."
Consequently, to advance this emancipation is part of the
Church's duty as cultural exorcist.

A second and third application is made to the field of sex
and to that of education respectively. Where the modern cult
of "The Girl" and "The Playboy" is in question, the exorcist's
role is quickly appreciated. "Both Miss America and The Playboy . . . represent the constant danger of relapsing into tribal
thralldom which always haunts the secular society, a threat from
which the liberating, secularizing word of the Gospel repeatedly
recalls it." But the threat from the tribe is matched here by
another from the town. The need for the exorcist is equally
apparent in the sexual immaturity of Puritan and Victorian
town culture. Cox cites the two-edged thesis of Gogarten: "The
German theologian Friedrich Gogarten states that the two most
serious dangers from which the Gospel must be protected are
(a) its being dissolved into a myth and (b) its being hardened
into a religion of Law. In either case it ceases to be the Gospel.
When we examine what has happened to the Gospel as it
touches the area of sex, it is evident that both of these dis-
tortions have set in." Finally, turning now to the secularization
of higher education, Cox argues strongly that the Church cannot
afford but to accept the "dechristianization" of the university, in

the sense of its emancipation from the parental responsibility which the Church formerly exercised. Paradoxically, it is only as thus liberated from itself that the Church, present in the Christian members of the university community, can perform the essential services of cultural criticism.

From the foregoing account of Parts Two and Three, we should have a fairly clear reply to the first of the two questions stated just a short while back: what should be the bearing of all this on the nature and role of the Church? If on the one hand our treatment has been necessarily brief and summational, on the other at least the main lines of the reply had already been drawn, by anticipation, in the sections preceding, and to which we were able to give more detailed attention. We come, then, to the second question: How should it affect our concept of God?

But here Cox lets us down—though we say this only in half seriousness, since letdown is not exactly the right charge when it is the extraordinary complexity of the problem, rather than any carelessness or lack of scholarship on the part of the author, that leaves this final part of the study unfinished, in fact scarcely more than begun. The attempt is made in Part Four, in its single chapter, the last in the book, and entitled "To Speak in a Secular Fashion of God." But the discussion only repeats what has been said already. As a conclusion to the work, it is satisfactory, but not as a response to the question about God. In the Afterword contained in *The Secular City Debate,* moreover, Cox himself admits as much: "Finally, I came to the issue which has fascinated me most since the publication of *The Secular City.* It is the one dealt with in the final chapter, entitled 'To Speak in a Secular Fashion of God'. I concede that this chapter does not fully accomplish its purpose." He adds immediately: "My only defense is that the failure is not wholly mine but is shared by the entire theological community. For years the doctrine of God in theology has become more and more problematical. We have ignored or passed over it, but our sloth has now returned to haunt us. It serves us right, I think, that our shirking the work we should have done on the problem of God has now produced the widely celebrated 'death-of-God' movement in theology which, if it makes no constructive contribution toward extricating us from the quagmire, dramatizes with chilling cogency the bankruptcy of the categories we have been trying to use."

Someone reading between the lines here would gather that not even in this subsequent Afterword is Cox himself able to advance this particular question any further than he had in *The Secular City*. And the impression, in our view, would be quite correct. Cox is obviously still looking for a breakthrough. And this is brought out once again in his review of Leslie Dewart's *The Future of Belief* in the September, 1966, book supplement of *Herder Correspondence*. What Cox himself would like, would be a sort of "sociological" or "socio-historical" concept of God. But he is blocked by not knowing what to do with what has always been called the divine transcendence. It would be easier, in a sense, if he could simply banish this element as an unwanted distraction; if he could, for example, simply dismiss Chalcedon and refuse any longer to recognize it as posing a meaningful problem in contemporary Christianity. In the Afterword, there is a hint that he might be tempted a bit more in this direction than he had been when writing *The Secular City*. On the other hand, he may only be wanting to underscore the ideal of an absolutely free and unprejudiced inquiry. In any case, what he had left us with in *The Secular City*, and this is the item which remains to date the only sufficiently expanded statement to allow for judgment, is quite clear: on one side, a desire to speak exclusively of the human Jesus of Nazareth conceived in broadly sociological, historico-cultural categories; on the other, a real, if nevertheless unstressed, desire to affirm Chalcedon—

he actually does so explicitly—and to come to grips, eventually, with the difficulty Chalcedon continues to present.

When all is said and done, then, it is the first question, and not the second, that Cox has answered. We began our own examination of this study by seeking to determine what precisely, if anything, Cox added to the Bonhoeffer insights, and to these same as reformulated by Robinson. We have come to the conclusion that an addition, a very clear addition, has in fact been made. For Cox, the thoroughly "this-worldly" Christianity has its authentic foundation in the strictly spiritual, Christian, and Gospel creativeness of the secular forms. Anonymity, mobility, the defamilialization of work, the bureaucratic organization, diversity, pluralism, pragmatism and profaneness—in short, the entire setting and perspective to which progressive urbanization and secularization give rise advance at one and the same time the Gospel ideal of personal freedom and socio-cultural responsibility.

And Cox says more than this. Historical evolution not only moves in the same direction *as* the Gospel, but *from* the Gospel: for the town culture had not really been able to shake off the more serious retarding influences of the tribal residue, and the still later transition to the modern technopolis did not really become a concrete possibility, until historical culture received its fully Christian emancipation. The argument here is expressed with emphasis. In the Afterword, it is actually intensified: "When I turn to those parts of *The Secular City* I would affirm even more emphatically today, the first would be the basically positive evaluation of the process of secularization. Today I feel more strongly than ever that the secularization should not be viewed as an example of massive and catastrophic cultural backsliding but as a product of the impact of the biblical faith itself on world civilization." As we have ventured to comment before, however, it is at this point that Cox may be too Christian rather than not enough so. That the biblical faith exerted a great, even extraordinary impact on world civilization in and through the Christianization of the West, cannot be denied. But Cox wants to make it the uniquely decisive factor, and this would be much more difficult to establish.

In our judgment, then, Cox is on conspicuously firmer ground when he argues simply the sameness of direction. For this he does well. He isolates for analysis the basic forms of which urbanization and secularization are made, then draws out of each of them an innately spiritual and specifically Christian definition. The key to the definition is, in every instance, the compound principle of freedom and responsibility. This is the ultimate direction of the Gospel; but this is also the ultimate direction of the shaping and stylizing energies of secularization.

Behind this controlling insight, or perhaps better as part of it, there is a deep sense of evaluational optimism. For Harvey Cox, the world *is* getting better and better—and *spiritually* better and better. This is the only verdict one can return after a careful observation of what was achieved in the line of personal and socio-historical maturation as the tribe became the town and the town the technopolis. Yet, if Cox's positive verdict is absolutely clear, not less so are the distinctions with which he would have us understand it. If he is an evolutional optimist, he is far from being a naïve one.

First, in no sense does Cox ignore or minimize the "other side" of contemporary existence. Slum living, racial violence, the threat of world-wide atomic conflagration—all of this is very much a part of his total context. And one of the finest sub-chapters in *The Secular City* is that taken up with "The Church's Diakonic Function: Healing the Urban Fractures."

Secondly, even when Cox is about his chief task—drawing out the spiritually creative and strictly Christian definition of what makes up the shape and style of the secular city—he is always careful to add that there is nothing automatic here. Anonymity can depersonalize; but it does not have to. Mobility, if anything more easily, can promote rootlessness and irresponsibility, but should not and need not. The "organization," perhaps most obviously of all, is fraught with the great risks of a brand new enslavement, though there is no reason why such risks cannot be met and controlled.

In a very important paragraph in the Afterword, Cox balances very soberly the pro and the con: "Still, the process of secularization is not an unqualified good. I wish to affirm a direction in history, even a process of evolutionary differentiation in the history of religion. But I want to avoid a simple 'progress view'. Here the image of the crap game, which I originally borrowed from Archie Hargreaves and which drew numberless comments, both positive and negative, will help. I would argue that secularization 'raises the stakes' of the game. It puts man in a position where he can do more harm and more good, where his mistakes will be costlier and his virtues will be more salutary than ever before. Secularization means increased control by man over his physical environment, deepened knowledge of his own inner workings, mightier weapons, more powerful medicines, higher aspirations, the need for more accountability. The secularization of the world is a summons to man to grow up. He can still refuse. But his refusal in our time would be incomparably more catastrophic than in any previous period." This is why back in *The Secular City* Cox had referred to secularization as "a dangerous liberation."

Secularization, therefore, does not purify or save automatically. Its forms can be misappropriated. On the other hand, it would be wrong to judge that in the final analysis secularization is a mixture of good and bad, or a thing that can go either way. For in Cox's view, the evolutionary process which he is describing is understood as good and spiritually creative in its ideal. If he does not wish to endorse a naïvely progressivist interpretation of history, he nevertheless does wish to affirm what he calls "a direction in history." In the ideal, maybe it would be better to say more simply in principle, the forces of secularization enlarge the opportunities of freedom and responsibility. And they do so more and more as time goes on.

It has been our personal experience while lecturing on these themes that someone in the audience will almost always want to argue that Cox's optimism is refuted by one obvious fact, namely, the progressive breakdown in morality throughout the modern world. But we find ourself very much on the other side. It is not that there are no difficulties! The universal breakdown as it seems to be envisioned, however, concentrates strongly on, for one thing, sexual morality, and in so doing tends to ignore other things that are of much greater importance. To make the picture really complete, we would have to consider, for example, the evolving attitude on such serious matters as capital punishment and the justified war. Those who are critically, and not just emotionally, opposed to both exhibit the ever deepening appreciation for human life. But so also do those who may continue, in an equally critical spirit, to allow both, but give evidence at least of recognizing the ultimate gravity of the problem far more than had our thirteenth and even nineteenth-century ancestors. We would likewise have to consider, still to make the picture really complete, the evolving attitude on such further matters as international and personal liberties, the constantly growing and articulated respect, in principle certainly, for the sovereignty of even the smallest states, and for the civil rights of all groups within any given nation.

In our view, then, Cox's thesis is profoundly valid: the Gospel and the world take the same direction.

In the context of traditional Christian theology, however, two further questions must be asked before we can conclude. And since the same two questions must also be put, as it were, to John Robinson, we can expand our critique to include once again both authors. The two questions concern first the "naturalism," and secondly the "immanentism," of the secularization theology.

The point of the first question is that Christianity is before all else a revealed religion. Its fundamental claim is that it did not evolve "naturally" from merely anthropological, psychological, socio-cultural and historical forces, but was communicated by God to man in the direct, in a sense interventional, manner that is known as revelation. This does not mean, of course, that the merely anthropological, psychological, socio-cultural and historical did not exert a profound influence upon the Judaeo-Christian articulation and expression of the divine revelation. To deny such an influence, or to talk as though the divine revelation could be considered in some pure state and as capable of being isolated from the purely earthly and human forms in which it became incarnated, is absurd. It does mean, however, that the ultimately non-earthly, non-human, and strictly divine origin of the revealed communication is unequivocally proclaimed. A Christianity that would attempt to avoid this proclamation, therefore, would at least be a Christianity with a difference.

In *Honest to God*, Robinson faces the problem head on. He is quite aware that his sustained diatribe against "other-worldliness" could be taken to imply a naturalistic reduction of Christianity's claim to be revealed. In his final chapter, therefore, he explicitly entitles an important sub-section "Christianity and Naturalism." The discussion takes the form of a dialogue between himself and Julian Huxley, and Robinson emerges as the unreserved champion of the revealed character of the Christian faith. Apart from this, Christianity is simply nothing at all: "Christianity stands or falls by revelation, by Christ as the disclosure of the final truth not merely about human nature (that we might accept relatively easily) but about all nature and all reality. The Christian's faith cannot rest in the capacities of man." There is something, moreover, besides a mere admission here. For Bonhoeffer before him, Jesus of Nazareth was God's utterly unique self-identification. In Robinson's enthusiasm to follow Bonhoeffer, therefore, he is not only going to grant Christianity's revealed character; he is going to emphasize it.

As for Cox, we have already said enough on his understanding of the primacy of the biblical faith in the most decisive moments of historico-cultural evolution. One could use the expression "biblical faith," however, without meaning to suggest the context in which the element of divine revelation was presupposed. Does not Cox in fact reduce biblical faith to a merely historico-cultural force? And is this not precisely what is meant in this connection by naturalism?

Actually, Cox does not face the problem here so bluntly as Robinson, nor exactly as an anticipated charge of naturalism. On the other hand, his preoccupation throughout is to contrast not simply biblical faith, but the God of biblical faith, with all manner of counterfeit and imposter. Further, while seeking to locate the true Church Cox argues that we must first discover where "the action" is; but the action is divine, and it can be discovered only in Jesus by whom God is revealed. His words here deserve to be quoted: "The key to locating the action is, of course, that the same God who was there yesterday is present in the action today. To locate today's action we need to know the lead actor, and this actor has disclosed himself in the life of Jesus of Nazareth. As we noticed in discussing the Kingdom, here too the location of the action is a christological problem. After the action has been uncovered, when we know where and what God is doing, then we can ask about the appropriate shape and style of church life."

Now it is possible, of course, to gloss this text. The critic of Cox can reply somewhat as follows: "Right. Excellent. Only in Jesus of Nazareth, conceived as 'the man for others,' does one find God. Cox's God, that is: the ultimate symbol of socio-cultural authenticity." The idea would be that Cox's God is not the transcendent God at all. But such a gloss is not in any way justified. We mention its possibility, however, simply to show how the question about naturalism quickly turns into the question about transcendence.

But there is also another difficulty. We noted a short while ago that Cox may be too Christian rather than not enough so: in that he may be attributing to the direct impact of the biblical faith upon world civilization changes that really took place independently of that impact. If, then, Cox were someday to concede such an objection and modify his position, would not the consequence next be that what he had singled out as the thing specifically biblical, and therefore revealed, was really something natural all along? Or to put it a bit more concretely, does not Cox make the essence of the biblical revelation freedom and responsibility? He does—at least in a sense. Earlier, we explained that his doing so does not however conflict with the New Testament's assigning primacy to the ideal of universal charity. And now we have to point out that neither does his doing so conflict with Christianity's revealed character. For in the context of the naturalist objection, freedom and responsibility is both natural and revealed, not either the one or the other exclusively.

The ideal of freedom and responsibility is something that could have manifested itself to the human spirit, in the course of evolution, quite independently of the biblical revelation. In fact, it actually did so, to a significant extent certainly, and most likely far more than Cox allows. On the other hand, the biblical and especially New Testament revelation profoundly refined this ideal and deepened its meaning, as it found its perfect exemplification and realization in Jesus "the man for others." God himself, in Jesus, now authenticates the ideal. And God himself, in Jesus, achieves it as the fulfillment of salvation history. To have any merit, therefore, the further objection would have to call into doubt what Cox makes of Jesus; and so once more the question about naturalism turns into the question about immanentism and transcendence.

We move on, then, to the second question, that of the "immanentism" of the secularizationist theology. The point of this second question is that the God affirmed by Christianity is other than, and distinct from, his creation. In traditional terms, he is transcendent and he is infinite. The terms, of course, pose something of a problem: transcendence and infinity trace back to the hellenization of the primitive Church. And it is the belief of a growing number of contemporary theologians that the pattern of thought characteristic of that phenomenon can no longer communicate to the man of today. Both Robinson and Cox feel this way. Dewart is a more recent and more striking example. But even Bernard Lonergan seems to concede the reality of the problem at least to a certain degree. In a lecture entitled "Dimensions of Meaning," and presented at Marquette University in May, 1965, he states frankly that "classical culture has given way to a modern culture," and that "the classical mediation of meaning has broken down." Towards the end of the lecture, Lonergan at least notes in passing that the breakdown of the "classical culture" creates real difficulties for the philosophy and the theology which were articulated in the idiom of that culture.

On the other hand, we must be equally careful not to oversimplify here. Transcendence and infinity may well belong to hellenization and classical culture. As normally used by philosophers and theologians, quite clearly they do. But the affirmation of God as Creator, and the less sophisticated awareness of God as other, do not: for they go back to the very earliest period of the Old Testament tradition, and their "inter-culturality" suggests a noetic base far more broadly human. Hence, we can discuss the question of God's otherness and distinctness without here and now discussing any further the more particular question of hellenization.

Robinson, immediately after treating "Christianity and Naturalism," takes up "Christianity and Supranaturalism." And once again, the author of *Honest to God* is out to defend himself against an anticipated charge, this time the charge of immanentism. He begins by observing that "it is perhaps necessary to rebut rather carefully the suspicion of pantheism, which must doubtless cling to any reconstruction that questions the existence of God as a *separate* Being. For traditionally, the immanentist or pantheistic world-view has been countered in deism and theism with the assertion that the world owes its origin to *a* Creator, an almighty Artificer, who at a moment of time (or 'with' time) 'made' it 'out of nothing'. This is clearly a highly mythological and anthropomorphic picture. But it is entirely possible to demythologize it without lapsing into pantheism."

Negatively, therefore, Robinson formally renounces any immanentist or pantheistic world-view. Positively, he embraces the doctrine of creation, and the concept of God as Creator, provided, of course, that both of these be corrected, or demythologized. From the rest of the section, and from the whole context of *Honest to God*, it is clear what has to go; but it is a great deal less clear what has to take its place.

Robinson is not attacking the otherness and transcendence of God as such. He is attacking only the particular concept of otherness and transcendence which represents the projecting and objectifying penchant of religious imagination. "But the projection of God *from* the world as a super-individual is no more necessary an expression of transcendence than is mileage upwards from the earth's surface. They are both but objectifications in the language of myth—in terms of 'another' world—of the transcendental, the unconditional in all our experience. The test of any restatement is not whether this projection is preserved but whether these elements are safeguarded. And that I believe I have tried to do."

The restatement referred to is in terms of love and freedom, but it does not quite succeed. In place of the materialism and determinism of pantheist philosophy, Robinson calls upon the interpersonal relationship of love and freedom which is the mark of true creationism. The transcendence of God can be seen only in the context of the *I-Thou* analogy and perfect freedom, with however the addition that the freedom of the creature is a freedom of dependence. One difficulty in all this is that Robinson now introduces an emphatically "personal" notion of God, whereas earlier this is precisely what he seems to have rejected. What he rejected, however, and continues to reject even now, is the notion of God as *a* being, and, from what is implicit in the passage cited just a moment ago, *a* Creator. On this first point, therefore, there does not seem to be any real inconsistency.

Nevertheless, there is a more serious difficulty with the overall value of the restatement as restatement. Traditional Christian philosophy and theology has no more time than Robinson for a concept of the otherness and transcendence of God supplied from the context that is set up by the single number of the indefinite article. The same traditional Christian philosophy and theology makes no less than Robinson of the strictly and exclusively "personal" analogy. It is hard to see, therefore, that Robinson has added anything in his putative reconstruction. What he leaves us with, in fact, both in *Honest to God* and in *The New Reformation?,* is acceptance of creationism, divine transcendence, and even Nicaea's consubstantiality, on the one side, together with an ultimate failure to integrate these doctrines into his thoroughly "this-worldly" Christianity, on the other. When all is said and done, Robinson himself poses the problem of such integration, but then backs away from it.

Cox does the same thing. As we concluded just a short while back, he is quite successful in suggesting what should be the

specific implications of progressive secularization upon the nature and role of today's Church, but very much unsuccessful in
offering anything similar for the concept of God. And once
again, it is the problem of what to do with transcendence.

In sum, therefore, we have shown how both Robinson and
Cox—but Cox especially—have made serious contributions to
contemporary Christian life and theology. However, before
leaving the present chapter, we would like to point out two
equally serious sins of omission.

First, the Robinson-Cox Secularization is without a theology
of death. It is a very excellent thing to insist, as both do, that
the Christian must not live in this world as though he really
lived elsewhere all the time. But it is a very mistaken thing to
give the impression, as both seem to do, that the Christian must
live in this world as though he were to live here forever—at
least in the sense that his destiny was exclusively orientated
toward the cause, even the highest spiritual and Christian cause,
of "this-worldly" evolution.

To be sure, both Robinson and Cox believe in an afterlife.
If Cox were thought to leave some doubt on the point, this
could be met, for example, by citing what appears to be his
notion of the Kingdom as at once temporal pilgrimage and
eternal fulfillment. But in neither of the two authors is the
affirmation of immortality, or better of the specifically Christian
resurrection from the dead, a truly operative religious or theological principle. The result is a grave oversimplification (pun
not intended), a lack of synthesis practical as well as theoretical.
It can, of course, be defended: one might retort that the need
to debunk the false imagination of "other-worldliness" is so
absolutely vital to contemporary Christianity, that an author's
total precision from a theology of death is here and now justified. But if such be the case, then the over-simplification and lack
of synthesis must at least be observed by others.

Secondly, the Robinson-Cox Secularization is likewise without an integrated theology of divinity and transcendence. Where Cox is concerned, we stated earlier that we had no desire to censure him for not having been able to give a satisfactory answer to his second question: How should all this affect our concept of God? But there is more to it than this. For both Robinson and Cox leave the impression that today's Christian must endeavor to identify with Jesus of Nazareth as "the man for others," and, as it certainly seems, without attention to his divinity. This calls for systematic comment.

In a sense, it is perfectly true that the New Testament itself does not focus upon divinity. "Divinity," unlike "Suffering Servant," "Son of man," "Lord," is not part of its immediate symbolism. Thus, van Buren is correct in arguing that divinity, as a piece of explicit theology, was introduced on "the way to Chalcedon." Robinson is correct in insisting that the New Testament exhibited a non-ontological alternative, so to speak, in its Word theology. Divinity, in short, is not what was immediate to either the thought patterns or literary expressions of the New Testament, but rather what is uniquely to be concluded from what was immediate once the question of divinity is raised— raised, moreover, in the language and cognitional structures of another and different culture. Hence it is that traditional Christian theology came eventually to speak of the divinity teaching of the New Testament as implicit rather than explicit.

On the other hand, however, there is the possibility here of a very serious and most uncritical oversimplification. Since the question of divinity was not explicit in the New Testament itself, since it became explicit only in the process of hellenization, the Christian of today may quite reasonably ignore it. But this is simply an anti-metaphysical romanticism. The man of today—the mature Christian, that is, and not necessarily the professional theologian—is born after, not before, the hellenization phenomenon. The third, fourth and fifth centuries are as much a part of him as the first and second. In fact, they are more a part of him than the first and second. If it is the peculiarly hellenic, and then Graeco-Roman style of thought which is had in mind, this was to become an almost infinitely more important ingredient in the cultural evolution of modern Western man than the Hebraic. Leslie Dewart's argument calling for a radical reassessment of what has been brought about by hellenization presupposes rather than refutes this fact. For the mature Christian of today, therefore, the question of divinity, precisely as the question of divinity, arises because it has arisen— and the context in which it has arisen is as much a part of him, and more a part of him, than the biblical. And this remains true, the historical conditioning, even if that part is currently fading into the background with what Lonergan calls the passing of the classical culture.

We introduced Dewart. Our personal contention is not that Dewart has not scored a valuable point. His has not at all been the kind of heavily emotional, intellectually uncritical assault upon hellenization that Mascall and even van Buren tend to ridicule. Rather, Dewart makes the observation that, whatever else one might want to say on the point, this much at least is true: our talk about every other matter has kept pace with evolution on into the twentieth century, but our "God-talk" became frozen in the fifth. Consequently, there is the legitimate suspicion of a religious and theological immaturity. The possibility has at least to be faced—even by those who might end up concluding that the cultural imbalance spotted by Dewart can be quite satisfactorily explained.

We also introduced Lonergan. Dewart's observation implicitly assigns an extraordinary measure of historical contingency to what was achieved in the period of hellenization and under its influence: to Nicaea's definition of Christ's unequivocal divinity as consubstantiality, for example, and to Chalcedon's determination of two distinct natures. But is it not precisely here that Lonergan would wish to demur? As of the time he had completed his Latin treatises on the incarnation and Trinity, including the 1964 revised editions of both, yes.

What would have been Lonergan's reply to Dewart in the works just mentioned, seems clear. Nicaea and Chalcedon represent, from two necessarily different points of view, both something relative and something absolute, something contingent and something necessary. If it was relative to the New Testament writers to speak of Jesus as Suffering Servant and Son of man, it was equally relative to the Fathers at Nicaea and Chalcedon to speak of Jesus in terms of being, and substance, and nature. But there was also something else. The transition from the descriptive and dramatic categories of the New Testament to the (broadly speaking) metaphysical categories of Nicaea and Chalcedon did indeed represent a passing from one culture to another. Within that trans-cultural movement, however, there was another. To think and talk of Christ as "consubstantial to the Father," is not to name him or describe him at the level of function and experience, but to understand him and in a sense define him at the level of cause. It is to pass from thinking and talking about things as they impress themselves upon us to thinking and talking about things as they are in themselves—to pass, therefore, from what is relative to what is objective and absolute. And it is here that classical theology reflected the essentiality and necessity consciousness of classical science.

True, it had always been characteristic of Lonergan's whole position to assign primacy in the activity of intellect to the spirit of inquiry, hence to leave the question open-ended. And this is the insistence Michael Novak echoes in his article entitled "The Absolute Future" appearing in the January 13, 1967, issue of *The Commonweal.* It remains, on the other hand, that up through 1964 (or a year or so earlier to allow time for printing) Lonergan certainly gave the impression of recognizing only a very restricted, and in a non-pejorative sense of the word superficial, contingency to the doctrinal formulations of Nicaea and Chalcedon. To use his own distinction, he appears to have judged the matter exclusively in the context and presuppositions of classical consciousness. But it is right here, as already noted, that more recently Lonergan has achieved a rather crucial breakthrough. For if the formulations of Nicaea and Chalcedon remain true in themselves, infallibly so, and Lonergan does not in any way suggest otherwise, something further may have to be said nonetheless as to their degree of relevance. And the reason for this is that from the human and psychological point of view they were product precisely of that classical culture which Lonergan now sees as gone.

The problem of theological reconciliation, therefore, in what concerns the hellenization of our "God-talk" is a serious one, and, in the writer's personal view, a still very much unsettled one. But this should not disturb us: the question has only recently been raised in its present context.

Having said all this, however, we would like to affirm once again that we must not make a simple identification between the problem of the talk about God, including the divinity or "the being God" of Jesus, and the much more specific problem of hellenization.

Thus, in talking about Jesus of Nazareth modern man quite certainly cannot *exclude* his being God the way van Buren does —not and still be a Christian in the sense of the Christianity of origins. What blocks him from doing so, moreover, is not in the first instance Nicaea or Chalcedon, but the primitive Christian confession "Jesus is Lord."

Can modern man, then, at least *prescind from* Jesus' being God the way Robinson and Cox do? Without denying that Jesus is God, but in fact actually asserting it, can modern man nevertheless concentrate exclusively on "the *man* for others," with perhaps the idea that divinity will sort of take care of itself? If this means not to make divinity the point of immediate and controlling emphasis, yes; he can and he should. For he sees God in Jesus, not Jesus in God. And in this connection it is perfectly legitimate to speak of a present-day return to the New Testament perspectives, priorities and formularies. Nor is sympathy for such a return by any means confined to the new radical theology. If it means, on the other hand, not to admit Jesus' being God into the totality of one's actual and activated consciousness—and to do so regardless of how theological opinion about hellenization and Chalcedon might someday come to be more sharply nuanced—then, no. The modern Christian cannot do this in practice; and the modern Christian theologian cannot dodge the task and responsibility of integration in theory.

The mature Christian must envision "the man for others" in an over-all context that has eventually to include his being God: not God, moreover, just as via a messenger, nor just as reflected in an image, but God strictly as *other*. This does not deny that he must see God as totally and uniquely self-identified in Jesus. God is totally and uniquely self-identified in Jesus, but *in Jesus* he is totally and uniquely self-identified *as other*. Jesus *is* Lord. In Jesus, God, the transcendently other, *is present*. Such must be the contemporary Christian's ultimate awareness, even if that awareness is not shaped concretely by the formularies of Nicaea and Chalcedon.

These latter, of course, he does not reject; but because of the profound cultural problem which we have mentioned, he may not recognize them as here and now meaningful. *De facto*, for example, they do not communicate to Robinson and Cox. For both Robinson and Cox, it is the same as saying that today's Christian must believe that God "came down from heaven"— literally, and without qualification.

Once more, therefore, we come back to a very real difficulty, that the solution, at least part of the solution, is undoubtedly the switch of emphasis to Jesus of Nazareth as "the man for others" —and with all that this implies, positively, for both Robinson and Cox. But it is precisely in this "man for others" that today's Christian must rediscover the God who is other than and distinct from his creation, not shy away from him.

IV.

The Future of Secularization

AN EARLY, but in its own way almost astounding, indication of how the valid insights of the Secularization movement will come to exercise a constructive and formative influence upon the institutional Church is the pastoral letter "The Servant Church" of Richard Cardinal Cushing, Archbishop of Boston, published on Gaudete Sunday, December, 1966. The explicit purpose of the statement is to reaffirm the teaching of Vatican II, and address that teaching in a practical way to world-wide, national and local problems. But the reaffirmation is also an extension, and the extension is in the direction of Secularization. The very title "The Servant Church," though it echoes the theme of two of the Council's most important utterances, at the same time gives to that theme a deliberately secularizationist turn.

After a brief introduction, the document sets out to "identify," in order, and as they should be conceived for the present day, Christ, his Church and the Christian.

Faithful, as we shall see in a moment, to the specific thrust introduced by Vatican II's *Dogmatic Constitution on the Church,* the Cardinal's letter identifies Christ as the Suffering Servant of God: "The central confession of faith in the primitive Church and in our own time is captured in the short formula: 'Jesus is Lord'. To confess the Lordship of Jesus is to affirm that Jesus still lives and continues his work, that the Lord who has been exalted (Acts 2:36) and who sits at the right hand of the Father (Heb. 10:12) still intervenes in our history, that he is, indeed, the Lord of history itself (cf. Col. 1:12–20). But Jesus we know is Lord only because he willingly and obediently endured the humiliation of the Cross, for 'though he was in the form of God, [he] did not count equality with God a thing to be grasped, but emptied himself, taking the form of a servant, being born in the likeness of men. And being found in human form he humbled himself and became obedient unto death, even death on a cross. *Therefore* God has highly exalted him and bestowed on him the name which is above every name, that at the name of Jesus every knee should bow, in heaven and on earth and under the earth, and every tongue confess that Jesus Christ is Lord, to the glory of God the Father' (Phil. 2:6–11). Jesus is Lord then because he is, first of all, the Suffering Servant of God. 'For the Son of man came also not to be served, but to serve, and to give his life as a ransom for many' (Mk. 10:45)."

The text from Mark is the same one that had been given a key role in the service motif of the Vatican II Constitution on the Church. But in the very next sentence, the Cushing pastoral observes that the Suffering Servant is synonymous with the "man for others" made so much of in theologians like Bonhoeffer, Robinson and Cox. These men are not named, nor is the Secularization movement as such. But the use of quotation marks to draw special attention to the expression "man for others," and to the word "secular" immediately following, and to the formula "religionless Christianity" a bit further on, leaves no doubt as to who and what is in mind: "Jesus came among us to announce the coming of the Kingdom of God, to give himself up for its realization, and to show us what it means to live an authentic human existence, to be a 'man for others'. What is most important to recall is that Jesus announced the coming of the Kingdom, not in abstract, purely religious terms, but in the thoroughly 'secular' manner foretold by the prophet Isaiah (Is. 35:5–6; 61:1)."

Next, the letter identifies the Church as the Servant Church precisely: "The Church, we know, is the Body of the Lord, but she cannot share in his exaltation until she has followed with him in the path of humiliation and suffering service. Jesus is Lord because he is, first of all, the Suffering Servant of God. So likewise is the Church the Body of the Lord because she is, first of all, the Body of the Suffering Servant of God. She is a Servant Church. . . . To see the Church as the Suffering Servant of God, ministering to the world for the sake of the Kingdom, is an insight of first importance for all of us. It is, as we have seen, eminently biblical, and it also underlies the whole perspective of Vatican Council II. For we must insist that the Church has no other purpose but Christ's: 'to give witness to the truth, to rescue and not to sit in judgment, to serve and not to be served' (*Church in Modern World,* n. 3; cf. nn. 40 and 45). The concern for service is also clearly evident in the discussion of authority in the *Constitution on the Church,* where the Council insists that every member of the Church must exercise his authority in 'the service of [his] neighbor' (n. 40; cf. nn. 27, 28, 29 and 41). As the Lord was the 'man for others', so must the Church be 'the community for others'."

Thus the pattern of the Cardinal's letter becomes still more clear: reaffirmation of the service ecclesiology of Vatican II, plus a partial, but deliberate and bold, appropriation of the Secularization emphases. This same pattern is continued in the third and last identification, the identification of today's Christian as "servant and healer." To specify service as the service of healing and binding the wounds precisely, as the letter does at this point, is to second the very strong motion made by Harvey Cox; but no less is it to follow to the letter the *Pastoral Constitution on the Church in the Modern World.*

It is here, moreover, that Cushing's pastoral introduces the patently secularizationist terms of "religionless Christianity," the "other-worldly," "secular city," and, with the meaning special to the present-day movement, "religion": "In a sense, the Christian of today *is* being called upon to adopt what some have called a 'religionless Christianity'. This is certainly not a Christianity without God, or Christ, or the Church, or worship, or the sacraments, or prayer. But it does mean leaving behind that narrow concept by which 'religion' is often known in our time. This is the notion that religion is purely 'other-worldly', that it has nothing to do with the 'secular city', that it is simply a matter of individual taste and preference, that it is concerned only with the sphere of private morality and ethics, that it has no place in the social, political, or cultural areas of life. This is a 'religion' incompatible with true Christianity. It is in this sense that some modern theologians, on both sides of the Reformation-divide, have called for a 'religionless Christianity'—and it is *in this sense* that we can agree with them. For the Gospel comes uncomfortably close to life. It is addressed to *this* world and it is meant to be applicable to the needs of this world. The Gospel calls upon us to heal and to reconcile, to serve and to bear witness—here-and-now, in this world."

To appreciate the full significance of the Cardinal's albeit reserved and qualified approbation of the Bonhoeffer themes, however, we have to situate his stand in the context both of more recent Church history and of much older Christian tradition.

At the close of Vatican II, there was throughout Christianity an air of optimism and success. One of the chief reasons for this was, of course, the great experience of Christian unity in and about the Council. Not everything was perfect. Countless sectarian differences remained: in doctrine, in forms of worship, in the very notion of the Church. But Christians were at last in dialogue, talking with one another, and setting out to work together for the Christianization of the modern world.

Yet, it is right here that someone could have seen a brand new difficulty, and a far greater one than that of the slowly healing Christian disunity: the ecumenical dialogue was very much intramural. *Within* the Christian community, now becoming conscious of itself precisely as the Christian community, there was indeed conversation and cooperation. *Outside* the Christian community, on the other hand, Christianity itself was not really in conversation with the secular world: with business, with science and technology, with megalopolis and the secular humanism. And this, when all is said and done, is the observation of the secularization theology.

It is important, moreover, not to misjudge—in either direction —the "secular," as distinct from the more strictly "ecumenical," accomplishment of Vatican II. The *Pastoral Constitution on the Church in the Modern World* had a great deal to say *about* the world, business, science and technology, and the secular humanism. And the prevailing attitude, notwithstanding words both of caution and criticism, was extremely positive. At the end of the fourth chapter, a sort of conversation *with* the world as an ideal to be sought for seems to have been implicit in a consideration of "the help which the Church receives from the modern world." Yet, conversation *with* the secular forms was not expressed as already achieved. Nor could it have been. Between Christian and Christian, there was dialogue despite differences because behind the differences there was explicit awareness of a more profound unity. But between Christian and secular man, there was at best only the desire for dialogue, and precisely because the greater unity was as yet nebulous and unarticulated: in a sense, the conversation was still only a sympathetic monologue.

Yet, if Christianity is going to talk with the secular city— and with it, not to it, much less at it—we must not minimize the obstacles. For Christianity includes in its basic symbolism a sharp division between "the things of God" and "the things of the world." We can trace this right back to the New Testament: for example, to the cenacle discourse in the Fourth Gospel. And we can trace it through a two thousand year tradition of Christian asceticism.

It is not surprising, therefore, that even Vatican II spoke at times haltingly, almost patronizingly, about the worldliness of the world. Thus, in the opening chapter of the *Pastoral Constitution on the Church in the Modern World,* where the subject at the moment is the mystery of death, we read: "All the endeavors of technology, though useful in the extreme, cannot calm [man's] anxiety." This, of course, is perfectly true; and we have already noted as one of the gravest weaknesses of Secularization its lack of a theology of death. But "useful in the extreme," though it is a refreshingly positive expression, is nevertheless not quite the way one might be expected to speak if he saw the relation between technology and Gospel, as Cox does, as a real dialogue. In other passages of the same document, moreover, there is considerable emphasis on technical progress as responsible for depersonalization and dehumanization, and in the discussion on atheism this latter is very clearly attached to the secular, earth-bound, new humanism of our generation.

No less surprising is it, therefore, that scarcely a year after the closing of the Council, and as evidenced by Cardinal Cushing's pastoral, the Church seems to be coming to talk about "the world" a bit more precisely—just as in Vatican II itself the Church had come to talk more precisely about heretics, schismatics and non-Roman Catholic Christians. It is not the world as such that is evil, nor its "shape" and "style" and "form," the "form" generated by science and technology, but simply man's misuse of these gifts—and it seems that in the future the Church will start saying so more frankly.

On the one hand, then, Vatican II, at least in one group of its utterances, continued the Church's age-old negativist manner of speaking about the worldliness of the world. But this is only half the picture. For on the other hand, Vatican II, in another and parallel group of its utterances, exhibited a far more positive attitude toward the world, in a sense even the worldliness of the world, than had ever been seen in the entire history of the Church. More than this still, Vatican II, as the pivotal element in its revised ecclesiology, openly encouraged the faithful, beginning with the hierarchy, to identify with a Christ conceived precisely as the Suffering Servant. And what is significant about this, is that the Christ so conceived, the Suffering Servant, is synonymous with "the man for others," which is the concept of Christ advocated by Bonhoeffer and the theologians of Secularization.

If Vatican II left an important nuance to be inserted later by Cardinal Cushing's pastoral, Vatican II at the very same time nevertheless laid the basis for this insertion in its service-concept both of Christ and his Church. This was a new step and a vast step. The fact can best be brought out by contrasting the Church's self-image achieved in Vatican II with that which had been created a little less than one hundred years earlier in Vatican I. The essential point of this contrast is the introduction of the service symbolism.

On July 18, 1870, Vatican I defined the infallibility of the Pope, and did so in a document entitled, just like its counterpart of a century later, the *Dogmatic Constitution on the Church.* The earlier statement was considerably more brief, consisting of a preamble plus four concise chapters, each of these concluding with an anathematizing canon. The Introduction set down the reason for the Church's existence, which is to perpetuate the work of redemption; and the reason for the Church's hierarchical structure, which is to preserve all the faithful in one faith and unity. Next, in quick succession, Chapter One delineated the establishment of the primacy in Peter; Chapter Two its continuation in his successors; Chapter Three the nature and extent of the papal authority; and Chapter Four defined the papal infallibility. The whole tone of the document was canonical and austere, with the prevailing emphasis upon the rights and power of the hierarchy.

In an article on "Freedom, Authority, Community," which appeared in the December 3, 1966, issue of *America*, Fr. John Courtney Murray, S.J., comments on the same document. In the immediate context, he is speaking of the attitudes shown by Leo XIII shortly after Vatican I, but with direct bearing on the Council's Constitution on the Church: "[Also] there is Leo XIII's ecclesiology, as summed up, for instance, in the encyclical *Satis Cognitum* (1896), in which he says: 'we have faithfully depicted the image and figure (*imaginem atque formam*) of the Church as divinely established'. The encyclical is, in effect, a lengthy, profound, magisterial commentary on the Vatican I constitution *Pastor Aeternus*, which was the splendid sign of the theological times. The portrait of the Church that emerges is really a portrait of the role of the apostolic office, and in particular the Petrine office, in the Church. In consequence, the ecclesial relationship—to call it such, on the analogy of the political relationship—is the simple vertical relationship between ruler and ruled. The function of the faithful appears simply as obedience to the doctrinal and jurisdictional authority of the Church."

But Vatican II, in *Lumen Gentium*, changes all this entirely? No. Nor is this quite Murray's point either. In fact, Vatican II in *Lumen Gentium* goes out of its way to make it absolutely clear that it is not reversing any of the positive teaching of Vatican I in *Pastor Aeternus*. Thus we read in the introductory first paragraph of the later document: "Since the Church is in Christ like a sacrament or as a sign and instrument both of a very closely knit union with God and of the unity of the whole human race, it desires now to unfold more fully to the faithful of the Church and to the whole world its own inner nature and universal mission. This it intends to do following faithfully the teaching of previous councils." The observation is expressed generically, but it is Vatican I and *Pastor Aeternus* that is really in mind. The second paragraph in the third chapter, "on the hierarchical structure of the Church and in particular on the episcopate," removes all doubt: "This sacred council, following closely in the footsteps of the First Vatican Council, with that council teaches and declares that Jesus Christ, the eternal Shepherd, established his holy Church, having sent forth the apostles as he himself had been sent by the Father (Jn. 20:21); He willed that their successors, namely, the bishops, should be shepherds in his Church even to the consummation of the world. And in order that the episcopate itself might be one and undivided, he placed Blessed Peter over the other apostles, and instituted in him a permanent and visible source and foundation of unity of faith and communion. And all this teaching about the institution, the perpetuity, the meaning and reason for the sacred primacy of the Roman pontiff and of his infallible magisterium, this sacred council again proposes to be firmly believed by all the faithful."

In other words, the assertion of undiminished continuity is actually backed up by a point by point repetition of Vatican I's formal teaching. On the other hand, there is just a bit here of the person who "doth protest too much." Vatican II took great pains to affirm that it was not reversing Vatican I precisely because that impression could have been given. Vatican II was changing something and knew it—not the formal doctrine of Vatican I, no; but nevertheless the whole larger context into which that doctrine would now become absorbed.

Concretely, Vatican II in *Lumen Gentium* no longer begins from and with authority, but subordinates authority to service. The bishops have authority, but only that they might serve the community, and do so, moreover, modelling themselves precisely upon that Christ who "came not to be served but to serve, and to give his life as a ransom for many" (Mk. 10:45, as in *RSV*). Thus we read in the third chapter, the chapter on the bishops: "A bishop, since he is sent by the Father to govern his family, must keep before his eyes the example of the Good Shepherd, who came not to be ministered unto but to minister (Mt. 20:28; Mk. 10:45), and to lay down his life for his sheep (Jn. 10:11)." This means that the Christ upon whom the bishop must model himself is Christ conceived precisely as the Suffering Servant. But the Suffering Servant is "the man for others."

A moment later, speaking now of priests, *Lumen Gentium* continues: "Priests, prudent cooperators with the episcopal order, its aid and instrument, called to serve the People of God, constitute one priesthood with their bishop although bound by a diversity of duties." Actually, the Christ of Mark 10:45; the Suffering Servant, who is the same as "the man for others," is introduced right from the fifth paragraph of the first chapter; and this service motif runs throughout the entire document. Further, in *Gaudium et Spes,* Vatican II's *Pastoral Constitution on the Church in the Modern World,* the motif is both sustained and translated into the area of practicality.

In the article just referred to, Murray makes something of the same observation we have been making ourselves as to the profound change introduced in this respect by Vatican II. It is part of his discussion on the concept of community, with which, of course, service is closely linked: "It may be fairly, if rather broadly, said that Leo XIII comes to the notion of the Church as community through the notion of the Church as society. . . . Authority seems, as it were, to stand over the community as a power to decide and command. In contrast, Vatican II comes to the notion of the Church as society through the notion of the Church as community. Authority therefore stands, as it were, within the community, as a ministry to be performed in the service of the community." And we must add immediately: for such was the authority of Christ, the model, the Suffering Servant, "the man for others," who gave everything he was and had in order to serve.

When all is said and done, therefore, it is Vatican II that has paved the way for the eventual incorporation into the institutional Church—in the first instance, but not exclusively, into Roman Catholicism—of the creative insights of Secularization. The Council has done this, concretely, through two distinct but clearly compenetrating movements: first, by assuming throughout its pronouncements a vastly more positive approach to the world as such; secondly, by centering this more positive approach, Christologically and ecclesiologically, upon the specific symbol of the Suffering Servant. Today, with the rapid growth of studies in linguistics and communications, no intelligent person is going to dismiss lightly the significance of a shift in basic symbol, or argue that no matter what be the name, the title or the concept under which Christ is conceived it remains the same Christ. It is the same Christ, of course, but not in the sense intended by such an objection, not in the sense that any change or difference would be "merely accidental." For there is an important law of reciprocity here: the Suffering Servant, or "the man for others" symbol is precisely the one, and to a degree the only one, that today's secular humanism can first tolerate, and then, hopefully, embrace; it is at one and the same time, therefore, both the Christ that the world suggests to Christianity, and the Christ that Christianity proclaims to the world. It is, moreover, the *Pastoral Constitution on the Church in the Modern World* itself that early in the second chapter of Part Two, and in one of its most remarkable passages, points to the operation of such a law: "In every group or nation, there is an ever-increasing number of men and women who are conscious that they themselves are the artisans and the authors of the culture of their community. Throughout the world there is a similar growth in the combined sense of independence and responsibility. Such a development is of paramount importance for the spiritual and moral maturity of the human race. This truth grows clearer if we consider how the world is becoming unified and how we have the duty to build a better world based upon truth and justice.

Thus we are witnesses of the birth of a new humanism, one in which man is defined first of all by his responsibility toward his brothers and toward history."

Equivalently, this passage in *Gaudium et Spes* affirms the sameness of direction principle articulated by Cox: if not with respect directly to what Cox calls the "shape" and "style" of secularization, at least, and most certainly, to the new humanism which he sees as emerging from this "shape" and "style," and to its ideal of freedom and responsibility.

Index